Even Pirates Go to Heaven

Even Pirates Go to Heaven

By Cindie Roussel

Thibodaux, Louisiana

Even Pirates Go to Heaven
By: Cindie Roussel

Published by: Cindie Roussel,
Thibodaux, Louisiana. 70301
www.piratesgotoheaven.com

Unless otherwise indicated, Scripture quotations are from the Revised Standard Version of the Bible, copyright © 1946, 1952, and 1971 by the National Council of the Churches of Christ in the USA. Used by permission. All rights reserved.

Hemingway, Ernest – The Sun Also Rises, Copyright ©1926 by Charles Scribner's Sons. Copyright renewed 1954 by Ernest Hemingway.

This book is a true story, however some names and details have been changed to protect the identity of those who appear in the pages.

Cataloging-in-Publication Data is on file with the Library of Congress.
ISBN-13: 978-0615979519
ISBN-10: 0615979513

Published in the United States of America

This book is dedicated to you, Blake.
I miss your laughter and that big beautiful smile.
But most of all, I miss your HUGS!!!
I love you, Mom

Even Pirates Go to Heaven

Acknowledgments

The stories in this book are from many friends and family members who shared the little time we had with Blake, my son. Some of these stories are even written by Blake from his early college days. He was commonly known to some as BT or Captain BT.

Blake always had a story of fun, trouble with the law, women and drinking. It was always an adventure. Blake never had a dull moment in his life. He believed that you lived everyday as though you were burning daylight. Somehow I believed he knew his fate. He must have known that he had only a little time and he was going to make sure his time was well spent. He could never get enough time in a day. If you were with him, you were in for a good time no matter what. You might not know where you end up, but you could expect a good time to say the least.

Thank you to his many friends and especially to those who helped me through the tears. Thank you to the volunteer divers and the USCG Cutter Pelican Crew for coming to our aid in helping us try to find Blake. Thank you, Kathie, my sister for being my rock. Thank you to my wonderful children and grandchildren who kept me going and most of all, to my loving husband for your arms that held me through the most difficult time in my life.

I love you all,
Cindie

The following people contributed to this book by sharing their personal stories, memories, and dreams about Blake. I appreciate their support and willingness in helping me keep Blake's spirit alive!

Allen (Jr) Gautreaux, Jr.
Allison Brown
Angelle Baudoin
Candace Wade
Derrick Rotolo
Dustin Terry
Jared Uhlich
Jesse (Joose) Lagarde
Jessica Brown
Jonathan (Nobile) Nobile
Korte Cheramie
Lance Parker
Lauren Slowik
Mary Baudoin
Meryl Marx
Maloy Guilbeau
Natalie Davidson Riddell
Nicholas (Ponce) Toups
Randy (Boudreaux) Boudreaux, III
Reesa Gravois
Ross Armstrong
Russ (Weazal) Guidry
Sara Dumal
Thomas (Deke) Brown
Tyler (T.C.) Cheramie
Whitney Terry Fletcher
Chad Breckenridge – Cover Photo

Special Thanks to my editors:
Debbie Daigle, Paul Sylvest, Wendy Folse and Whitney Terry Fletcher

Prologue

"Mah, it's me…Blake." I was in shock as I held the phone to my ear. "Blake, where are you?" I shouted. "Do you know that we thought we lost you in the Gulf?" "Yes, Mom, I know. I don't remember what happened. All I know is that I went to sleep and I woke up at a camp in Lake de Cade." His voice was so calm, as though he wanted to try to keep me calm. There was static on the phone. His voice kept fading in and out, "Mah, the connection will be hard for me but I will keep trying to reach you, okay? I am working down in Cocodrie, and I will let you know where I am headed next."

I could hear voices in the back-ground. He seemed to be distracted while he was speaking to me. This was not unusual for Blake, as he always had twenty million things going on at one time. "Can you come home?" I asked, knowing in my gut the answer already. He paused and then he said, "No. I have work to do, but just know I love you, Mah. I love you very much. I will keep in touch so don't worry, okay?" He told me one more time, "Mom, I love you."

THEN I WOKE UP. Tears were flowing down my face and my heart was pounding. This dream was so real, that when I woke up, I had been crying in my sleep. I woke up Scott, my husband and I told him of my dream.

The night before, I told him that maybe it was time to shut-off Blake's cell phone. I had left his phone as it was the day he went missing. I left both his voice mail and his text messages alone. I did not have the heart to shut it off. I could still call it and hear his voice and I did not want to lose all that we had left of him. Scott put his

9

arms around me as I laid there crying and he said, "We need to keep his phone on just in case he calls again.

Preface

Cocodrie, like Fourchon and Grand Isle, is located in one of the most unique and beautiful places in the world, south Louisiana. Located 90 miles southwest of New Orleans, it is an hour and a half journey on a scenic two lane highway filled with common sights of trawl boats along the bayou, signs marked "Crabs, live or boiled," and of course that deep flat Cajun accent that deepens the further south you go. The smell of shrimp and salty air from the Gulf is prevalent along this flat land. Every time you travel towards the Gulf, you wonder just what took you so long to come back.

For Blake to tell me that he was working down in Cocodrie, this was not unusual for him. He spent his life traveling from Lafayette to Grand Isle repairing boat motors and taking care of customers and friends boats between his fishing adventures. He loved the water and that was usually where you would find him. He called Port Fourchon and Grand Isle, "God's Country." He believed there was no other place better than the Gulf of Mexico for fishing.

To wake up at a camp in Lake de Cade was Blake's way of reassuring me that he did not die in pain. He fell asleep something that can happen to divers when the deep depths cause their air to become poisonous and mix into their blood stream. I am grateful that he could reach out to tell me. We were very close, as close as a mother and son could ever dream to be. Our connection, no matter if he is in the spiritual dimension between earth and heaven, I know will remain close.

This book is not just about Blake, but about hope and believing that the miracles that are handed to us every day are not just coincidental.

Through each of the stories you will learn that everything Blake did in his life was not just by accident, but was part of a bigger plan.

Chapters

Even Pirates Go to Heaven

Chapter 1

The Accident

By Cindie Roussel

My day was no different than any other day. I had worked all day on my patio and had just returned home from the local hardware store with a table and set of chairs. Scott was fishing for the first time in a long time. As I poured a glass of wine to relax and to start putting together my patio table, the phone rang...

Nobile: "Ms. Cindie, it's not good. Blake did not surface. We were making a dive at 160, 180 feet down and we were coming up together and then I shot a fish. I looked back and I did not see Blake."

Cindie: "What do you mean, Nobile?"

Nobile: "It's not good, Ms. Cindie, all I saw was bubbles, so I followed them but I could not find him. I went another way to see if he was around the platform and then I went to the top and started screaming his name."

Cindie: "Nobile, what do you mean he did not surface??? I can't breathe...I can't breathe, Nobile."

Nobile: "Ms. Cindie, who is there with you?"

Cindie: "No one....I CAN'T BREATHE, OH MY GOD...I CAN'T BREATHE!"

This was the worst night of my life. Nobile proceeded to tell me that they had called the Coast Guard, but I could not comprehend what he was saying to me. All I could remember was that I could not catch my breath. All the air had just vanished in my lungs and I could not breathe. I called my neighbor, Necole from the house phone while I kept Nobile on my cell phone. She came over and wrote down the information from Nobile while I sat there just numb. Earlier, Jared Uhlich had called me on my landline to check on Blake. Jared and Blake had made many dives together. They wore their equipment just alike. Jared would say that looking at Blake in the water was like looking at himself in the mirror. He told me that he had a weird feeling in the pit of his stomach as Blake was not answering his cell phone. I remembered telling him not to worry, Blake is offshore and his phone is probably not working.

Within a few minutes of hanging up with Jared, Nobile called. I had to dial *69 to get Jared's phone number as I did not have his number. Jared became my center point of pulling the dive team together. My house became headquarters for search and rescue of Blake. I remembered calling Scott to get home as quickly as possible. I called Dustin, my son and Necole called Whitney, my daughter. Then I realized that I had not called Rachel. Rachel was Blake's girlfriend. She was pregnant with his child and they were planning to celebrate the announcement of the baby's gender the following Tuesday. I don't remember much except her voice was so low and calm. I knew the shock had hit her as I too could not fathom what I was saying. This was so unreal to me. She asked if he had been drinking. Maybe this is just him being stupid and he is on a rig close by…but I think she knew like I did that this was something he would never joke about. This was real and we did not want to have this conversation.

Little did we know where our journey was leading us that day. We had no clue what to expect.

We were not prepared for such a loss. We feared the unknown and we had no clue what to do next.

Nobile, Me and Blake

"With my whole heart I cry; answer me, O Lord!" Psalms 119:145

Chapter 2

A Pirate Is Born

By Cindie Roussel

I can remember having all three of my children at the boat shop, back then called the Bayou Sporting Goods. This shop is on the west tip of Ocean Springs, Mississippi just before the Ocean Springs and Biloxi Bridge. Blake's Grandpa, Chester Terry ran an outboard motor repair shop on the side of a Sporting Goods Shop. Billy Anderson ran the Sporting Goods Shop. Chester was a tall handsome man with big blue eyes and white hair. He was a righteous man; well respected by the community as a loving husband and father. He married Mary Lee Murray February 9th, 1947. Mary Lee (Grandma), was a French woman who had dark hair with brown-eyes who was not afraid to speak her mind. She was a strong Catholic woman and believed that there was no other faith but catholic.

Together they had seven children, Chester Jr., Henry J., Curtis, Michael (Crockett), Rose Marie, Cheryl Ann and Anthony Mark (Tony). They were a very close knit family. It was impossible to not be consumed by their passion to be together, sharing their love for life. Tony and Crockett both worked for Mr. Chester in the boat shop. Every Friday night, they all gathered at the shop for crawfish, shrimp or whatever was plentiful in season. The shop was full of motors and parts with usually a grease rag sitting on a table where one of them had just been working on a power head. Lower units lined the outside with boats backed up to the door. It was there that Tony was usually stretched over the back of a motor turning a wrench. Come 6:00, the distinctive roar from the propane gas burner under a pot could be heard. The aroma of crab boil filled the air as laughter could be heard coming from inside the shop.

There stood Mr. Chester with his back tall and straight, draft beer in one hand and a big cigar in the other. They had a beer keg that he had rigged up to an old refrigerator. There were folding tables and metal chairs set out where there was plenty of room for whom ever showed up. There was never a guest list or invitations sent out because if you saw the shop door open, you were invited. No matter how cold it could be outside, the shop was always warm and inviting. It was a place that everyone loved to gather. It was not anything fancy, but that did not matter as there was always plenty of food and love in that little shop.

I married Tony in October 1983 and Blake was born March 21st 1984 the following year. Blake Anthony Terry was a week old when I brought him to his first outing at the shop. Everyone passed him around while I sat down to already peeled crawfish as Mr. Chester believed in taking care of the ladies. I felt special when I would go there as I was treated like family and I knew I was loved.
Shortly after, Dustin Mark and Whitney Scarlett were born. I toted each of them in baby seats with diaper bags to the shop for Friday night gatherings.

Blake was driving a tractor and backing up boats before he was 3 years of age. He could back up a boat even though he could not reach the gas pedal, of course the tractor was always idled high enough that you did not need to press the gas to go forward or backwards. Tony was not a patient individual, but when it came to trusting instincts, Blake and Tony had the connection. Blake would look directly at Tony and he did exactly what he said

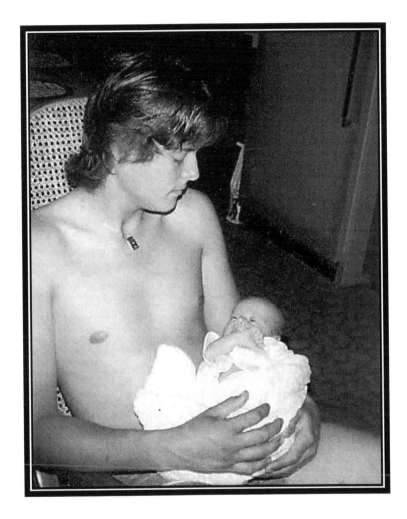

Tony and Blake

Chester, Mary Lee and Blake

Tony was a master mechanic and between Blake and his father, they were a dynamic team when it came to outboard motors. Crockett took a lot of time with Blake and helped him learn the details of working on motors. He was patient and he made sure Blake understood.

When it came to Tony, he was constantly fixing motors. Even on weekends when we were headed to the islands, I can remember someone was always in need of help. It was no wonder Blake followed his footsteps as the water was his life and he had a special calling when it came to being a boat mechanic. Blake was still in diapers when he would go to work with Mr. Chester and Crockett at the shop. Mr. Chester would bring him home at lunch time to change his diaper so that he could go back with him. Of course, they did not have pull-ups back then or he would have been wearing them.

Blake and Dustin

I can remember one time, Mr. Chester pulled up in the drive way earlier than normal. He said that Blake had a bad diaper and he could not take it anymore. Looking back, Blake should have been out of diapers by then, but he was hard headed and he was not easy to potty train. Blake pleaded with his Grandpa not to leave while I changed his diaper. I could not change him fast enough before he took off running back into Mr. Chester's arms. He did not even give me a kiss. He just waved and told me goodbye and that he loved me.

Things did not change after that. Blake was rooted in his love for family and the importance of working hard. He also learned to enjoy what was important. He was humble in his accomplishments, and thankful for all of the gifts God had given him. He worked hard to give back for the blessings he had been given. Blake was constantly running with no time to stop. His very last words to me on that Thursday before he went missing were the same as back then, "Bye Mah, I love you!"

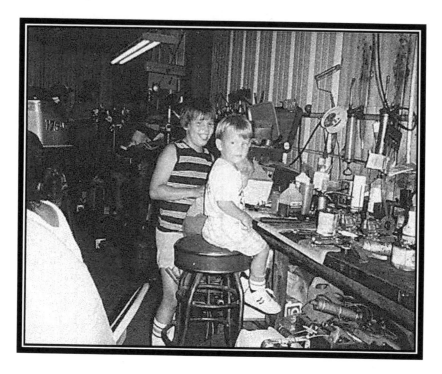

Blake and Joey, his cousin

Chapter 3

Do You Believe?

By Cindie Roussel

Although it was not in Blake's character, not many folks knew about Blake believing in fairies…yes, he believed in fairies. He was probably 5 or 6 years of age when he experienced something that I will never forget. We were visiting Aunt Happy, my older sister whose real name is Kathie. Blake had trouble saying Kathie, so he called her Aunt Happy and it has stuck with her ever since. He was good about having nicknames for everyone. I guess you could say that she was the 1st to get a nickname.

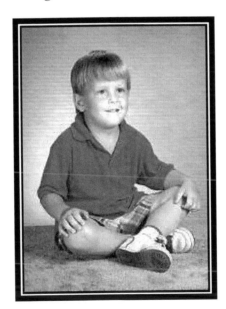

Blake

We were sleeping over at Aunt Happy's and Blake had lost his first baby tooth. That night he placed his tooth under his pillow anticipating the tooth fairy's arrival. Aunt Happy and I were still up talking in the living room when Blake was supposed to be sleeping, however he came running out of his room white as a ghost. He was trembling as he said, "Mah, I did not move. I was scared, but I did not move." I looked at him puzzled and I asked, "What were you scared of?" He said, "The tooth fairy." "The tooth fairy", I asked. "Yes," he said. "She was sparkling with wings and she was green. I did not move. I was scared. I waited for her to leave," he said shaking. He laid still in bed and waited for her to leave before running to tell me.

Tony and I divorced in 1988 and I followed my career, moved my family to Savannah Georgia. In 1991 we relocated to a quiet town in Louisiana, called Lockport. We moved into a little house in the back of Nolan Toups subdivision, on Romy Drive where my children were embraced by a ton of friends. They were involved in just about every sport and activity that was available.

I was a single parent living on a modest income. I would usually cook smokies and mac-n-cheese on Friday nights for supper. After dinner, we would move the coffee table and play music to dance to. I taught each of my children how to couple dance as well as how to jitterbug. We would dance the night away until early into the morning. Some might say that those Terry kids could dance...or at least they thought they could.

In 1995, I married Scott Roussel. He swept me right off my feet. We both worked together but really never talked to each other at work as he was the warehouse manager and I was the logistics manager for a local shipyard.

Cindie, Blake, Dustin and Whitney

One day I asked him if he could give me some old boxes in order to make a boat out of the cardboard for a skit Whitney's youth cheerleaders were doing that following Saturday. Instead of giving me the boxes, he offered to help. Next thing you know, Scott was coming over on Friday nights helping me make signs for the football games. One special night, he asked if he could kiss me good night. I was stunned. I never believed that I could ever be happier in my life than at that moment.

Later in life, Blake still believed that he saw something, whether it was actually the tooth fairy or maybe an angel, I may never know. I am sure he never shared that with his buddies, as I am equally sure there are many things he shared with them that I will never know either.

But to me those untold stories are the best stories and memories that we all have in our hearts. Whether they are believing in something that you have never seen or the visions of the unknown or just dancing your feet off because you have nothing better to do, they are special impressions in our hearts that will live with us forever. We will never forget that moment as it was so real to him. Was it really a fairy? Or, maybe it was his guardian angel, only he knows now.

Dustin, Scott, Whitney, Me and Blake

"Lo, sons are heritage from the Lord,
the fruit of the womb a reward."
Psalms 127:3

Chapter 4

Raising a Pirate

By Cindie Roussel

Both Blake and Dustin played football and baseball. They loved sports and being at the ball field was our social life. Each played position of catcher in baseball. Blake was left handed but he played ball with his right. He could nail second base every time. He was quick and fast. He was so good at throwing the ball that the coaches tried him several times at pitching, but the poor players would get so beat up as he just never had enough control of the ball for that position.

Blake

Whitney cheered at the youth football games and she just went right into cheering in school. They were all so involved. They tried every sport, but I think football and baseball were our favorite times.

One day we received a call from the school that Dustin had gotten into an accident in the lunch room. They asked if we could bring him a change of clothes. Dustin and Blake both attended the junior high school, three miles south of where we both worked. Our house was just a mile down from the school, so Scott left work to go by the house and bring Dustin some clothes. When he got to the school, Dustin was covered from head to toe with chocolate milk.

Dustin was in sixth grade and a ninth grader had poured milk on his head during lunch. Scott was not happy as he put his hand on the back of Dustin's neck and could feel the dried milk. He took Dustin home to shower and put on some clean clothes. Scott brought Dustin back to school and then headed back to work. Later that day, we got another call from the school for both of us to come up as they had an issue with Blake that needed to be discussed. I thought, GREAT! Blake found out about Dustin and probably got into a fight with the ninth grader.

When we walked into the principal's office, Blake and another little boy were sitting across from the Principal. Scott and I looked at each other and thought okay, they must have gotten into a fight. The principal began to explain that they had an investigation going on in the school and found drugs in several students' lockers. My heart went to my stomach. Blake is in eighth grade. How could this happen? I kept thinking "his life is over!" He is too young, my sweet innocent little boy who loves his mother. Look at him sitting there, with those sweet big blue eyes, I thought, "someone must have put pressure on him. Kids can be cruel and someone must have threatened him because he would have never done something like

36

this. There must be a mistake!" and then WHAM!!! The principal's door flies open and out of the blue comes the other little boy's mother. She was a large black woman who they must have called at work because she was still in her work uniform. She flew over the principal's desk and started beating the crap out of her son. Blake jumped out of the way while Scott and the principal pulled her off of her child. She started yelling at him, "This is what I work two jobs for? So you can buy drugs?" She was screaming at him and the whole time Scott is holding her back from killing him. Blake is in shock at this point trying to climb over the back of the sofa and I am sure he was thinking, "This woman is going to kill me next!"

Finally, after the principal gets everyone to settle down, he starts again about the investigation. Blake had bought marijuana from the little boy and he was the only one that had not brought it to school. He admitted buying it so the school had notified the police. Blake told them that he had the marijuana in his locker at home. We didn't know any better at the time as this was the first for us. We should have asked for an attorney or some kind of legal advisor, but no; we all went home and got "the marijuana" out of his locker and then brought it to the police department. None us thought, "what if we get pulled over while heading to the police station?" We were so nervous and mainly in shock. Blake was in eighth grade; are you kidding me? He was too young to be messing around with drugs, or so I thought.

Reality hit when the principal expelled six students with the exception of Blake. Because Blake did not have it at school, they really could not expel him. However, the school banned him from any sports activity which devastated all of us. Blake loved football and he was good at it. He had played centerline since his youth football days and we envisioned him playing for high school in the next two years. I had to do some fast talking. I called to meet with both of his coaches to try to arrange a deal. They both agreed to meet with us but made it clear that it was out of their hands. We sat down in our living room and I did the talking. I told them both that Blake held a 4.0 GPA. He was very smart and rarely did he have to study or work hard at school assignments. The only way that Scott and I could keep him out of trouble was sports. He had to play sports as the adrenaline rush playing on that field would overcome any kind of drug. He loved the game and he needed to play as much as they needed him. I further explained that not giving him a chance to work for something he wanted so badly would only discourage him later life. They needed to have a recovery plan for young pirates like Blake who screw-up. He was a bright kid who did not have to work hard at his studies and he would be bored if he did not have something to keep him out of trouble.

After several hours of me talking, they finally agreed. We laid out a plan for Blake to be drug tested every two weeks at our expense. That gave the coaches the physical proof that Blake was not using drugs. As for the other students and players, Blake would run laps before and after practice showing the students that he was paying the penalties of doing drugs. In reality though, Blake knew what he wanted and he was not afraid to be publically humiliated for doing something wrong. His desire to play football was so important to him that he did not care what others thought. He loved the game. He loved the fight. He loved being on that field. In the game of life, some of us are players while others are sitting on the sidelines too afraid of what others may think. Blake was not afraid; he loved the game too much to sit on the sidelines.

Blake
(Learning the sacrifices as a Pirate)

"I remember the days of old, I meditate on all that thou hast done; I muse on what thy hands have wrought." Psalms 143:5

Chapter 5

The Band of Brothers

By Blake Terry

"The Band of Brothers"
Nick (Ponce) Toups, Allen (Jr.) Gautreaux, Blake (BT),
Randy (Boudreaux) Boudreaux III and Jesse (Joose) Lagarde

The spring of 2002 began warming the air temperature early that year. At least that's what it seemed to be to me. Spring break was around the corner and my buddies and I started to prepare for what we thought was going to be the greatest time ever. Everyone was in the best mood because high school was almost over and the partying

41

was out of control way too early. We arrived in Florida and the beer drinking went a little over the limit that night. So the next morning everyone was feeling a bit sick. A few of us made our way to the breakfast table and managed to get some food down because we knew it was going to be a long day ahead of us. At least I thought we were in for a day of drinking on the beach and enjoying the beautiful scenery. Jr is a longtime friend of mine who I went to high-school with. As soon as we opened our first beer, while we were throwing the Frisbee in the front parking lot of the hotel, the man of the hour pulled up in his black and white hotrod. He was of course the good ole Florida police.

He proceeded to check our ages on our driver's license to see if we were old enough to be drinking alcohol. Jr. and I were the two obviously not old enough because my loudmouth put both of us in a bad situation. The young cop slammed us two in hand cuffs and shoved us into his backseat. He certainly made himself a nice hero on his radio once he was bringing two young criminals to the jail house. Jr. and I still kept on talking with our smart remarks as if we were invincible.

Once we arrived to the police station, things became worse. The car ride to the front gate was hard enough to try to remember since we were tourists. We had no idea where we were or who we were going to call since no one knew how to get to the station. The cop was not very cooperative since Jr. and I weren't cooperative ourselves in the first place.

He proceeded booking us and made us put our belongings in a container on a rack. This rack was next to the door of the jail cell we were put in. We had to dress in a very comfortable prison outfit and into the tiny jail cell we went. The cell was the nastiest and grossest room and was very unsanitary. It had a toilet and a ten inch bench seat that was just too short to lay your back on. We thought it was pretty horrible, but we figured we would only have to spend maybe an hour in.

Little did we know, we sat in that room for nine hours. During the time we were in it, we had to listen to everyone who tried to get in touch with us because the cop left our belongings next to the door. Finally, our buddy that put us in there decided to let us free. We were both very hungry by the time we were let out since we only ate breakfast that morning. We walked out of the back door of the place and had to hitch-hike our way back to where we were staying.

Blake and Jr.

We both had a shorter stay that year, and it ended up costing the two of us more than we thought the trip was worth. It was two thousand to total the fines up. We arrived home and were definitely not the happiest people about the whole situation. We learned that the work we had ahead of us was not equal to the beer that put us in the bind we were in. We both had to work extra hours until the end of school or we were not allowed on our senior trip. We thought we were invincible since we were younger at the time and about to graduate high school. It made us look at situations different and not be as irresponsible as we were that time. It taught the two of us a lesson because we thought we couldn't be touched and the law proved us wrong. It also made us appreciate our money more because our parents would not help us pay for any of it since it was our own stupidity.

"When you're in jail, a good friend will be trying to bail you out. A best friend will be in the cell next to you saying, "Damn, that was fun". Groucho Marx

Chapter 6

Have You Lost Your Mind?

By Cindie Roussel

When the kids were little, we use to ride around in my blue Pontiac playing 1980 songs. Back then, Blake's friends really had no clue about my generation of music. Playing the Eagles or Jimmy Buffet music was what I loved to listen to. Little did I realize the impression this music would have on Blake's life. "A Pirate Looks at 40" by Jimmy Buffet was a true look into what Blake's life was. Blake seemed to be born late in life by the family values and traditions he believed in. I also believe that he somehow knew his fate from that he would die at a young age. He always said that he would never live to see himself grow old. I can remember a few weeks before he died, we were sitting on his porch and he told me, "Mah, I have done a lot of stupid things in my life. I have pissed so much money away just enjoying life, not to mention the trouble with the law, but you know what? I don't have any regrets. Each and every thing that I have done was a life experience. I loved every minute of it." I remember feeling so at peace with him on the porch that day. I thanked God as I knew at that point he had finally reached the age of his life that he was ready for the next chapter of his life.

Blake was not an easy pirate to raise and that is putting it lightly. From the very beginning, he was always in trouble. I use to tell him that having to come up to school every year to speak to his teachers or principal was a sign that maybe he had the problem, not them. I was always open with my children and we pretty much talked about everything together. The one thing we enjoyed the most was music. Riding around in my little car, we would turn up "Why don't we get drunk and screw" or "Pencil Thin Mustache" by Jimmy Buffet. Probably not the mother image like June Cleaver from "Leave it to Beaver" but I felt it was important to laugh and sing out loud, even if the songs might not be G-Rated.

Blake, Dustin and Whitney

Being open like we were, I just always thought that if my kids were tempted to try drugs or do something that they thought was wrong, they would tell me. What was I thinking? Then one day, I went to pick-up a bag of clothes that Blake had left at Randy's (Boudreaux) house and his dad met me at the car. He said that he wanted to inform me that he found a bong in Boudreaux's room and that it was Blake's. He wanted to have me talk with Blake as he did not want Blake influencing Boudreaux into doing drugs. I nearly died. Of course, this was Boudreaux's story when he was questioned about the bong and as a parent; you want to believe your child. You do not want to believe your child would be doing drugs or would be the one pushing others to do drugs.

What would my friends say, I thought? What would the school say if they found out? What about his sports? He would not be accepted into any college. He will end up on the streets pushing drugs or in jail! All these images were running through my head. Oh my God I am a horrible mother, I thought! My blood was boiling at this point. I had all these visions that my child was headed to hell.

I raced home to find Blake asleep in his bed. OBVIOUSLY, he must be stoned I thought. I yanked him out of bed and threw him against the wall. Now, Blake was 6 foot tall and about 175 lbs. He was playing center for high school football at the time, so he was not a small frame, mind you. I was every bit of 4 foot 11 inches and 100 lbs of PISSED OFF! I threw him as hard as I could and ripped into him about doing drugs. I will never forget that look on his face as I held him pinned against the wall. He was in shock and his arms were up in the air. He hollered, "MAH, HAVE YOU LOST YOUR MIND?"

I guess as parents, sometimes we lose it. I would say, that day I did. He could have picked me up and threw me across the whole house, but he didn't. He loved me with all his heart and the last thing he wanted was to hurt me. He knew I was angry, hurt and most of all disappointed. Of course, he denied the bong was his and that Boudreaux ratted on him to protect the innocent. I never found out who the bong belonged to or who actually was the influence in introducing them to drugs. Was it someone at school? Was it a bully and they were forced to do drugs? Was it one of the guys in their group of friends? Or was it ME who introduced them to songs earlier in their lives that were not G-rated? If I had to guess, Blake would probably say, "It was YOU, Mom. It was all YOUR fault for letting us listen to your music back then..."

Boudreaux and Blake

Me and Blake

"How can a young man keep his way pure?" Psalms 119:9

Chapter 7

The Best 1-Hour Party Ever!

By Cindie Roussel

Blake and his band of brothers, Jr., Ponce, Boudreaux and Joose were always into trouble...or trouble just seemed to find them. Scott and I were planning to go to Biloxi one weekend to spend time with my family. Usually, we all would go, but for some reason, Blake insisted that he wanted to stay home. Boudreaux had invited all of them to stay at his house as they were planning a fishing trip. I was hesitant but decided to let him stay.

Ponce, Jr., Blake and Boudreaux

The story kept growing and growing about what they were going to be doing while we were gone, but I did not pay much attention as I just thought they were getting excited about the fishing trip. Then one morning, Dustin told me that there were fliers going around school "Party at Blake Terry's house, Saturday night." So I waited until Blake got up to eat breakfast before I decided to ask him about it. Ponce and Jr. were both sleeping over so I thought this was going to be interesting to hear what they had to say.

Blake and Ponce

I asked Blake, "so I understand there is going to be a party here this weekend?" Blake choked a bit on his breakfast and looked at both Ponce and Jr. and then told me some kind of story that someone was playing a joke on him at school. That someone had printed those fliers and spread them all over school. They all reassured me that they were not having a party but they were going fishing. Suspicious, I contacted Jr.'s mother, Olga and asked her if she would keep an eye out to make sure that nothing happened while we were gone. Jr.'s family lived on 5ᵗʰ street off of Romy Drive and we live across from 10ᵗʰ street. Although we lived close to each other, our houses were still far enough apart that you could not see our house from theirs.

Come 7:00 Saturday night, Olga decides to take a ride down to check on our house to make sure the boys were actually staying at Boudreaux's house. When she walked out her door, the cars were lined up for blocks. She started to shake as she could not believe her eyes. When she pulled her car on the side of our street, she was in complete shock that she put the car in park and left it running.

There were kids everywhere. All were drinking and seemed to be having such a great time. As she eased the front door open, the lights were turned out. When she flipped on the lights, kids scattered like roaches. Someone hollered, "There's parents here!" She said they shot out the back door, some jumping off the rail of the back porch. She looked around and she did not see Blake or Jr. She could hear voices in the back room. She opened the door and there was a young couple in the bedroom. She told them to get out. Blake and Jr. finally walked in the back door. Both of their faces turned white as they saw Olga standing there with a disappointed look on her face. The party was over no sooner than it had begun. Blake and Jr. both always said that this was the best party they had ever had even though it only lasted for one hour.

"The steps of a man are from the Lord, and he establishes him in whose way he delights; though he fall, he shall not be cast headlong, for the Lord is the stay of his hand." Psalm 37:23

Chapter 8

The Great Dive

By Randy Boudreaux III

One day we were bored in Nolan Toups (the hood), when we decided to have some fun and pulled Ponce's trampoline close to his pool, which was an inground pool. We started doing tricks and grabs into the air into the pool. We were having a blast with it until Blake comes up with the bright idea to do a one and a half front flip into the pool. For one, the pool was only 3 feet deep at the end we were jumping into. For two, there is no way he was going to be able to shallow dive after pulling out of a tuck like that. But in Blake's mind he had it. So of course, there he goes, jumps and does a one and a half, pulls out of it and dives straight vertical into the bottom.

We all said, "HOLY SHIT!" He comes up holding his head saying "I think I chipped my tooth!" He takes his hand off his head and blood starts to trickle down his forehead. We look at his tooth and its chipped pretty bad. It almost looked filed. You could see the nerves. It looked like it hurt to me. We all jumped on our bikes and flew to Ms. Cindie's house. Blake was holding his mouth while blood was pouring down the sides of his head. When we got to Ms. Cindie's, all she could see was blood. She hollered, "BLAKE, YOUR BLEEDING!" She put his head in the sink and when he lifted up, he had a perfect scalped circle in the middle of his head. He had no hair in the center of his head. We all busted out laughing as he looked in the mirror at his bald spot. At that moment, he forgot about his teeth. He realized he would have to go to school with a scalped head and there was no covering that up.

Every time I would look at his big pearly white smile and see that slight discoloration on his front tooth, automatically in my imagination I can still see him doing the flip into the water and coming up licking his tooth saying I think I chipped it with blood running down his head. It's an image I will never forget.

Chapter 9

The Tank

By Randy Boudreaux III

Blake and I decided to get a job together our 9th grade summer. I really didn't want to but he was and I thought, why not? If Blake will be there with me, I might as well make some money. So that summer we were carpenter's helpers. Basically doing whatever we were told. Put up roofs, helped build walls, etc. One day when we arrived at work, our boss instructed us to hook up Blake's truck to a trailer full of wood. Blake had a Dodge Dakota extended cab with a v-6 in it. Most of our vehicles at the time were little extended cab trucks but only had 4 cylinders. So Blake's truck was a beast in our eyes. It could light the tires up all the way to third and bark'em on 4th! He had painted it a bright ass banana yellow, which I think he loved about it the most.

We hook up to the trailer and head towards the dump to unload the wood. We pass through the tunnel connecting the east and west side of Houma and in the middle of making it through the trailer starts to sway back and forth. We look at each other and Blake said, "I gotta speed up to correct it." Which he does and it corrects the swaying. We knew that was a close one. We drove to the other side of town and everything was fine. We were a couple miles from the dump and almost ready to complete the task when the trailer started swaying again, this time more vigorously and an even worse problem was that there were vehicles in front of us so we couldn't speed up to correct it. As Blake slowly hit his brakes you could feel us go one way, then hard the other way.

Blake and "The Tank"

You could hear the tires squealing as we made a complete 180 and rolled over in a little ditch on the side the road. I looked at Blake with the ground right by his head and he just lets out a big "AAAAHHHH!!" He says, "Get out man!" So I do, which the door was hard as hell to open because I had to push it against gravity and a door is heavy. Once I jumped out the door slammed right back down; then what I saw was slamming on Blake's big ass head. I heard him cursing like a sailor in the cab. I couldn't help but laugh a little. He finally got out the truck. We looked at what we called "The Tank" on its side and we looked at each other and said lets flip it back! Out of pure adrenaline, ole hammer head and me pushed and grunted the tank back on to four wheels just as people were coming up to see if we were ok. We looked at the side of the tank that was on the ground and the side mirror didn't even break off. It made an indention in the ditch and it didn't have a scratch on the side!!

"THE TANK!!!" we said. We told the people, "Nah we're good." Then we looked at the other side of the truck and the bed was kinked in half. We realized at that point, we didn't come out of this without any damage. But at least we were both ok and didn't get hurt, well except for a big bump on Blake's head from the door. All in all it was a learning experience. I now know how you shouldn't stack a trailer for sure. That was the end of our job that summer because the owner had to pay for the damages because he is the one that stacked the trailer in the first place.

"A true friend freely, advises justly, assists readily, adventures boldly, takes all patiently, defends courageously, and continues a friend unchangeably." William Penn

Chapter 10

Turn Mud into Sugar

By Cindie Roussel

Cane season in South Louisiana is something to see if you have never been in this area. Sugarcane has been an integral part of the south Louisiana economy and culture for more than 200 years.

The burning of sugar cane fields are a sign that fall is here. The reason the crops are burned is to remove mulch after harvesting so a new sugar cane crop can begin to grow. Although the sky is full of smoke, the smell is like no other. The air is filled with an aroma of sweet cane syrup. It is my favorite time of the year and it always reminds me of a story I must share.

One day, a sheriff's officer knocked on our door. He had court papers that someone had pressed charges against Scott. I thought, "WHAT? Scott has never even had a speeding ticket in his life, this is crazy!" Then he asked if Scott drove a Z71 with the license plate number that was registered in Scott's name. "No", I said, "That is my son's truck, Blake." Blake was being charged for simple criminal damage to property and vehicle. Here we go again, my blood boiling, images of him on the street or in jail the rest of his life. "He will be ruined," I thought!

Blake was dating a girl from Raceland, who the father of course, hated. I mean, he really HATED Blake and did not want him dating his daughter. She let Blake drive her jeep, which her father bought for her and the jeep was registered in his name. They took the jeep mud riding in the cane fields in the back of Gheens. They ended up flattening a tire while running over several stalks of cane. Blake fixed the tire and they cleaned up the jeep and brought it home like nothing had happened to it. Well, of course, the daughter confessed to her father what they did and he pressed charges. Did I mention that he really hated Blake?

I am not sure if any of you know the price of sugar cane stalks? They are not cheap! Each stalk damaged had a hefty fine of fifty dollars a stalk. We let our insurance agent handle the vehicle damages and as for the sugar cane damage, Blake did community service work as well as worked at the Raceland Raw Sugar Mill to pay back for the damages. Blake worked at the Sugar Mill for several years during harvest seasoning and by his senior year, he received a paid scholarship to Nicholls State University from the mill.

God really does have a plan, we just can't see it sometimes. We are always caught up in the moment, but never really see the bigger picture. Blake took those cane stalks and mud and turned them into sugar. God gave him the opportunity to turn a situation from bad to good.

Certificate of Scholarship

RACELAND RAW SUGARS, INC.

presents this

AGRICULTURE SCHOLARSHIP

to

BLAKE TERRY

Central Lafourche High School
May 23, 2002

Principal

Blake's Scholarship to Nicholls State University

"We know that in everything God works for good with those who love him who are called according to his purpose." Romans 8:28

Chapter 11

The Blue Torpedo

By Cindie Roussel and Randy Boudreaux III

When Blake turned sixteen years of age, Tony gave both Blake and Dustin a boat. I was mortified. I saw bad things to come. Blake was in and out of trouble with driving, and now you are going to give him a boat? Of course, I should have known better as Tony had a boat when he was Blake's age, so why not? All I thought was trouble, trouble, trouble. In order to make myself feel better, I told all the boys that they had to go to boater's school before they could put that thing in the water.

One Saturday morning, I loaded them all up in my minivan, remember, I was trying to cover up my real image by trying to look like June Cleaver. I had Blake, Dustin, Jr., Ponce, Boudreaux and Joose piled up in my minivan and off we headed to New Orleans to boaters school. That day, most of them slept during the entire class but me. I sat through the class and was attentive as I thought if they had any questions, I would be able to help them. I wanted to be that mom who knew so much about boat safety that they would respect me. When I gave them advice, they would think, "Man, she really knows her stuff, so we better listen to her." At least that is what I thought. When the instructor provided each of us our scores, I made the lowest grade in the class. That was the longest drive home as the boys ragged me the whole way home.

How the Blue Torpedo changed their lives
By Randy Boudreaux III

The Blue Torpedo was one of the best things that could have ever happened to us growing up. Since Blake's dad, Mr. Tony was around boats his whole life, I guess he thought his son should have the same. Blake was given the Blue Torpedo with a big ole motor on the back with a homemade ski pole that stood out the boat about 7 feet! It was perfect for hydro sliding and wake boarding. I remember one summer, Blake, Jr., me and so many other friends piled in the boat to go wake boarding and just have a blast. It would be an all-day affair. We would bring food, extra gas, and of course you can't forget BEER AND accessories!!

Blake and Boudreaux

The Blue Torpedo

We would ride up and down the intracoastal all day long taking turns doing tricks, trying to turn pro wake boarder; stopping in between sessions to jump off the occasional dry dock or high barge. It was always fun getting adrenaline rushes out of jumping off the high barges. We were out there literally every day one summer riding behind that boat saying that we're gunna turn pro. I remember we even went in the middle of December, when it was 50 degrees, because we just couldn't wait any longer. Two wet suits and a jacket couldn't make it any warmer though.

Blake excelled past me in the skills though. He had gotten a couple flips in his bags of tricks which definitely made him that much better than us. We were determined to become pro wake boarders. We had even gone so far as to make a proposal to our parents about getting us this bad ass wake board boat because if we had that we would be able to go pro. I still think to this day that have been the contributing factor, but the Blue Torpedo definitely got us as close as we could get.

We gotta give it up to the Blue Torpedo because without it we would have been some bored puppies those summers growing up.

**Blake, Jr., Jessica (Blake's cousin) and some friends in the
Blue Torpedo**

Chapter 12

Ship Island

By Jesse (Joose) Lagarde

Blake, Jr., Toby, Desiree, and I set out from Lockport on a Thursday headed to Mississippi for the Ship Island bash. We were ready for a weekend of fun but we didn't even make it to Boutte before we ran into trouble. We had a flat tire on the boat trailer leaving us without a spare. This never seemed to bother Blake as we were on a mission to get to the coast. We fixed the tire and hit the road. We finally made it to Grandma's house and proceeded to drink with Uncle Crockett in the basement. He cranked up his gravely and showed us how bad it was by cutting a trail in the woods only to get lost. We woke up the next morning with blazing headaches but Blake insisted we must push on!

We made it to the island with the sun beating down on us and we all felt like we were in paradise. We got the grill going, with horse shoes and radio cranking well into the night.

At around nine o'clock Blake and Jr. decided it was a good idea to head to the casino by boat while leaving us on the island. I swore to them not to go that they wouldn't make it back but they insisted. So off they went leaving the rest of us with a tent, a couple of drinks and a fire. THAT'S IT! We all finally passed out, no telling what time, without a trace of Blake or Jr. As we woke up in the morning, we found ourselves holding down the tent as a massive storm ripped through the island. It was like being sand blasted. Again, no sign of Blake or Jr! About thirty minutes passed when I finally heard a boat in the distance and I knew it was them because no one else would run in that kind of weather. Sure enough Blake was going so fast that he could not see the island and beached it right under us. I started cussing him telling him he should have never left and he went and got the damn boat stuck. Blake just turned to me and said, "Relax, it was all part of the plan."

Somehow we got the boat off the island and it cleared up and we proceeded to have the best day of our lives! We all made it back safely. I would always joke with BT when we turned 25 years old that we were in our mid- life crisis because all of the crap we had been through. I never knew how we made it that far! Blake is just passing the torch and we have to keep rolling. Looking back now, I realize that we learned from every story and eventually it would all makes sense!

Jr., Joose and Blake on Horn Island

"Relax, it's all part of the plan."
Blake Terry

Chapter 13

No Shirt, No Shoes, No Plane

By Cindie Roussel

Blake graduated in 2002 from Central Lafourche High School. He had a 3.6 GPA and he was headed for College. I can remember the week of graduation that he seemed like something was bothering him. When I asked him, he said that this was it, he was now an adult. He had to start making decisions of what he was going to do with his life. I think it kind of scared him a bit. That anxiety feeling of not knowing what you are going to do with the rest of your life. That did not last very long as college was a whole new world that Blake was not prepared for. PARTY, PARTY, PARTY!!!! His 3.6 GPA went straight down to a 2.0 GPA quickly.

Graduation was over and the boys were headed to Cancun, Mexico for their Senior Class Trip. I was a nervous wreck as they were going into another country and I was sure they would have trouble with the law. I helped Blake prepare all week. I sent off for extra birth certificates so that he had one packed in every piece of luggage as well as his wallet. I made sure he had plenty of money and I made sure he had a stash in each bag as well.

That morning he was ready to take off and he had everything he needed. My heart was in my stomach as I kissed him good bye at the airport. I told him to make sure that he had my number should he get into any kind of trouble.

All seemed okay and Scott and I had decided to go the Gulf Coast that weekend.

We were meeting family and we were in desperate need of some relaxation. We arrived on Friday night and things were going beautifully.

I had not heard from Blake as he could not call me on his cell, but I figured no news was good news, right? Wrong! My cell phone rings and I do not recognize the number, but my gut tells me to answer it anyways. I answered and it was an operator, "Will you take a collect call from Blake Terry?" He had been drinking and I could barely understand his words. He said, "Mah, what's my plane?" I said, "What?" He said, "What's my plane? You know my plane number? I'm at the airport and I don't know what flight I am on?"

I thought holy crap, how in the world are we going to go get him home? Who do I know that can fly me to Cancun tonight? I visualized him in a jail cell down in Mexico and I could not help him. Then I remembered I had put his information in my purse. I was not sure why but I had decided to keep it with me just in case. Good thing!

I told him his flight number and he should have already been on the plane according to his papers. He said, "I lost my wallet, ticket and bags. I was in a bar with a girl and she put me in a taxi to the airport. Everybody left me and I got to find Ponce." I was terrified. I told him to find his flight and call me back. Well he never called me back. My night was a long night waiting to hear back from him.

In the meantime, back at the hotel, Ponce had packed Blake's bags and brought all of his things to the airport. He was panicked as he did not know where Blake was and what he was going to tell me when he got home without him.

Ponce told me that they were boarding the plane when Blake walked up with no shoes, and no shirt but he had his arms out with the biggest smile. Ponce was ready to kill him, but Blake wasn't worried. He never seemed to be panicked or worried about missing that plane.

He was not going to miss one second of his time worrying about anything. He wanted to absorb everything he could up until the last minute before boarding his flight home. How ironic that he had the same attitude and zest for life right up until he died. He was not going to miss out on anything here on earth.

He was not worried or scared of missing his flight because he trusted God in his plan. I can only imagine how he felt when he saw Jesus. I envision Jesus with his arms opened wide, and there's Blake. His arms open wide with no shoes, no shirt, no plane, just THAT BIG BEAUTIFUL SMILE!

Ponce and Blake

Chapter 14

Search for Two Boaters Shipwrecked

By Cindie Roussel

Houma Courier - DULARGE
Published: Monday, August 16, 2004 at 11:34 a.m.-Rescuers searched by air and sea this morning for two boaters who went missing Sunday following a collision between two recreational vessels on Lake de Cade, a shallow body of water in western Terrebonne Parish. The wreck occurred sometime after 6 p.m. Sunday, resulting in the ejection of two men and a woman from one of the vessels, according to preliminary reports from the Terrebonne Parish Sheriff's Office and U.S. Coast Guard.

The missing were identified as Marvin Tre' Marmande and an unidentified man of Houma, both believed to be in their 20s. Two other people -- a woman ejected from one of the boats and a man who had not yet been identified by authorities this morning -- were rescued from Lake de Cade Sunday night.

The two boats collided in Lake de Cade approximately 10 miles southwest of Houma. The Terrebonne Parish Sheriff's Office and a helicopter from Coast Guard Air Station New Orleans searched throughout the night. Relatives of the missing men gathered at a Falgout Canal marina, from which rescue boats had launched through the night and which served as a temporary headquarters for law-enforcement personnel. They struggled with flagging hopes for safe recovery of the two men who remain missing while acknowledging that with each passing hour those hopes grew slimmer.

Lake de Cade, a shallow tidal water body, is a favorite and often crowded recreational-boating spot. According to officers searching at the scene, none of the people aboard the boats wore personal flotation devices. During the search, relatives of the missing men gathered at a Dularge marina to await word.

This was probably the hardest thing Blake had ever endured in his life. Tre' and Blake shared a college apartment at Nicholls State University and they became very close friends. Along with Tre', Blake met Ryan Blakely (Blakely), Jay Schexnayder (Primetime), Jonathan Nobile (Nobile) and Thomas Brown (Deke). Ross and Lance Armstrong grew up with Blake, but they really became close during college days. They were additions to his "Band of Brothers."

That evening I started receiving several phone calls from Blake's friends asking if Blake was okay. Blake and Tre' were always together. Everyone just assumed that Blake was on the boat with Tre' when the accident happened. The calls kept coming in and I kept telling everyone that he was in Mississippi. He was at Grandma's house in Ocean Springs. Then it hit me, "Blake does not know that something has happened to Tre', OH MY GOD! I HAVE TO GET TO HIM, BEFORE HE FINDS OUT." Jr. and Joose met me at my house. I kept calling Blake's cell phone, but he was not answering. We took off for Ocean Springs, which was about two hours away.

As we were just about to cross the Mississippi State line, my phone rang. Blake was screaming in the phone, "Mah, its TRE'....OH MAH, OH MAH....NO, IT CAN'T BE TRUE! I SHOULD HAVE BEEN WITH HIM, THIS WOULD NOT HAVE HAPPENED! OH, MAH....OH, MAH." He kept screaming my name and I could not comfort him. I could not get to him fast enough.

After we hung up the phone, I was speeding as fast as I could to get to Grandma's house. I called Henry Jay and Joey to go over there to be with him until we arrived. Finally when we arrived, he just wrapped those big arms around me and just fell apart. Tre' was like a brother to Blake, so when Blake told me (in my dream) that he was at a camp in Lake de Cade; the first thought that came to me was that he was with Tre'.

Losing your child tragically like Tre' and Blake is devastating. There are no words of comfort or answers to why something like this happens. All you can offer someone who is going through something like this is your arms. Holding them and letting them know you're there is all you can do.

Right after Blake died I can remember people telling me that life will be different. Life as you know it is going to be different. You will have to make new memories now. I can remember thinking, "WHAT? You have no clue what you are talking about? My gut has been ripped out of me and you are telling me life is going to be different?" In all honesty, people really don't know what to say or do in these types of situations. I just know that, "THERE ARE NO RULES" when losing someone you love. You never really ever recover.

I read this book right after Blake died to help me try to relate to Rachel's situation. There was a woman that lost her husband, of all things from a skateboard accident. He was skating and fell and hit his head. She was five months pregnant. The book was written from her own life experience of what she went through losing her husband and dealing with having to have her child alone.

I could relate to her feelings as I was in shock and it was almost a way for me to escape into someone else's life while my life was on hold. She would say that when someone would say something that just was crazy, like "At least he died doing what he loved." The first thought that came to her mind was "Shut the F*%k Up." Now I am not one to use the "F-word" but I could relate to her feelings. So forgive me for thinking the same thing but I just lost my son and the last thing I wanted from anyone was to tell me that I should be happy that he died doing what he loved!

I can remember Nobile asking me, "How does the book end?" Isn't that what we all want to know when we are hurting? How does it end? When will it end? How are we to go on living without our loved one in our lives? With so much pain, all we really want is just something to hold on to.

There are no answers to those questions. I just know that one morning I woke up and I could hear the birds outside my bedroom window for the first time since Blake had died. I knew then that I was going to be able to live again. I knew that Blake was fine and that I had to trust God enough to take care of him.

As a mother, no one could take better care of my children than me. So trusting God was very hard for me to let go, but I had no other choice but to trust him. I gave him my son and I now understood more of God's sacrifice of giving me his only son. What an ultimate sacrifice that he has done for all of us. The pain he must have endured. I understood. I have a different relationship with God now. I truly understand the sacrifice he made to give us eternal life. Blake and Tre' have eternal life now and I am comforted by knowing that they are together again.

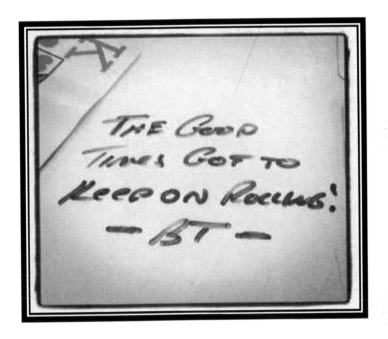

Chapter 15

Basic Chemistry

By Thomas Brown (Deke)

In the fall of 2004, I decided it would be a great idea to take a night class in Chemistry at the local college, but Professor Wong Lee thought different. Wong Lee was one of those that thought his class was above all things good and found pure pleasure in giving random quizzes at the beginning of class. I made B's on all of my tests, but Wong Lee failed me because of the quizzes and online work.

Anyway, me and this other guy were always late to class. The class was packed out and there were always two empty desks in the back waiting on us about fifteen to thirty minutes after class had started. I usually sat in the one across the far side with all the random people that we're interested in Chemistry and this other guy sat in the other empty desk that was perfectly positioned in this flock of good looking college ladies, naturally! So this one evening, about three weeks into the semester, I was late by fifteen minutes and my desk was taken but there were two empty desks in the flock, so I partook in having a seat with the flock for a change.

About five minutes later, the other guy shows up and sits in his seat. Thirty seconds went by and he says "hey man, did he give one of those pop quizzes tonight?" I said with a grin "hell, I don't know I only beat you by about five minutes." He smirked and grinned with that jackass eating a cactus look and said "hey man I'm BT." and stuck out his hand in which I shook and replied "I'm Deke Brown." Then he asked, "Why were you late to class?" I replied, "I've been alligator hunting. Why are you late?" BT replied "I've been spear fishing." At that moment I think we both knew that life was about to get better.

Wong Lee made up his mind he was going to fail both of us regardless of our grades because for the next hour BT and I discussed what we had been doing without ceasing from the five warnings Wong Lee had screamed at us that night.

After class, we walked down to our trucks to find we had the exact same truck. I found that pretty random, and we discussed all the same problems we had with them considering we both believed they were built to use as if they were army tanks. The rest of the semester BT and I would use the class to talk about our most recent and past adventures and mentally terrorize Wong Lee into second guessing his existence as a Chemistry professor. Little did Wong Lee know, but the basics of Chemistry happened about fifteen to thirty minutes after class had started. A bond was being formed to make a compound called "BT and Me."

I had been in South LA for about year and a half because of this lucky lady I was with and BT was one of the first true friends I had made outside of her friends. From then on, it was BT and me are going to do this and BT and me are going to do that. My girlfriend at the time was not so sure about the whole BT and me thing, which I can't blame her. It was great; when you became friends with BT it was like buy 1, get 12 for free.

Along came Nobile, Primetime, Jared, Joose, Johnny, Jr., and all the other crazies. The only person I brought to the table was my brother Jake who I guess was about as equivalent. Ha! We all had some good times. From the good old Team Skanktuary Days to taking BT duck hunt'n and frog'n for the first time and BT taking me spearfish'n for the first time, to our annual no holds bar Thanksgiving Hunt, gar holes, flounder holes, spearfishing, Grand Isle and Fourchon Trips, Thibodaux bars, Lockport Parade, and all the little things in between, it was a good time.

I had to get out of South LA for a while, but being the rambling sofa nomads my brother and myself are, BT and Nobile would always have a place for us to stay when we slid through town. If they were both out of town, Ms. Cindie would explain how to break into BTs house with a credit card so we could stay for the night at BT's anyway. It was like nothing had changed. We'd all get together and act like idiots and tell lies. BT and Nobile would bitch at each other like they we're married. Always Papa'n this and Mouse'n that.

Altogether, it would make me realize how much I missed South LA and what great friends we had become, much more like family. I am grateful that through life's turns, twists, flips and flops I got to hang out with BT in 2011. It's funny; I don't think he ever realized what an impact he had on all of us knew him. I don't think he knew that we all wanted to be a little more like BT. I told Jake laughing about it over the phone one day, in the early summer of 2011, that I needed to be a little more like BT. He agreed. I wanted to be that happy, carefree, helping, always grinning like I'd done something bad, and never hesitated to be nice to everybody almost as if to make it seem like they mattered and to help them have nicer day kind of mentality. BT was one of a kind, and I am very fortunate and blessed to say that I knew him and had the opportunity to hang out with him. I love being on the water, just like BT, and if you look close enough at the sparkle in a shimmer of water, whether it be on the bayou, river, gulf, bay, mud puddle, or even a glass of water you'll see that twinkle in BT's eyes when he's grinning, like I see every time.

Deke and Blake Frogging on the Bayou

Chapter 16

Hurricane Katrina

By Cindie Roussel

August 29th, 2005, Hurricane Katrina made landfall at 7 a.m. on the Louisiana coast between Grand Isle and the mouth of the Mississippi River. Days before, my nephew, Ryan (Kathie's oldest son) sent us updates telling us to get prepared. Ryan and his wife, Gina were working at the University of Alabama, both focused in meteorology. They were tracking the storm information and Ryan had the latest updates. The days to follow were unbelievable. My entire family lived on the Gulf Coast of Mississippi and Louisiana. Chris, my brother and his friend Tim lived right on the beach in Biloxi. The last words I spoke with my brother Chris were those of him swimming to a 2nd story house in D'iberville during the eye of the storm. He had to swim from one house to another to get to the second floor as the water kept coming. He said, "Sis it's bad. I will call you when it's over, if I make it."

The next several days were horrible. Not long after the storm hit, the unthinkable happened a large section of the 17th Street Canal levee gave way. Communications were difficult as cell phones, landlines, and power were gone. It was as though the world had ended that Monday morning. We were in Coushatta while Blake was in Texas with Tony. He wanted to stay close to home so that he could get back right away to help those in need. We started back home the minute the storm passed to find devastation beyond our wildest imagination.

As we came down the interstate, there were dead cows along the highway. The closer we got, the worse it became. You can only imagine the relief I felt as I pulled in our driveway to see our house still standing. We all met back at the house when Blake decided to take off to the coast to check on family. We loaded his truck up with water, bread, fruit and barrels of gasoline for the generators. He took two credit cards of mine and as much cash as we could come up with. He wrapped his arms around me with tears in his eyes as he said, "I love you, Mom. I am not sure how I will communicate with you, but I will try my best to let you know how everyone made out." He jumped in his truck with a pistol in his lap as the looting had already started. I prayed for his safe return as I cried goodbye.

The day grew long as I waited to hear from Blake. Finally, I started getting voice mail on my phone. Crazy as it may seem, the phones were not working but voice mail was. Each voice mail message was Blake. "Mah, I just arrived and Uncle Henry's and Aunt Carolyn's house, they're okay, Mah. I am now headed to Aunt Cheryl's and Uncle Ty's. I will call you from there." "Aunt Cheryl house is destroyed, Mom, but her and Uncle Ty are okay." "I am headed to Grandma's then Aunt Linda's and Uncle Curtis. I love you, Mom."

With each message I felt relief as he was reaching me with good news that everyone was okay. "Mah, Aunt Happy and Uncle Wil are okay. Their house is still standing." I felt relieved after each message. Wilfred said that they were in shock. They could not believe the devastation around them. They had no power, no water and no communication and then this kid pulls up in this big truck with barrels of gasoline, water, food and supplies. There Blake was with this big smile and open arms. Wilfred said the one thing he remembered the most about that day was Blake's big hug. He knew that everything was going to be okay after that.

As Blake left each message, I could hear in his voice the tears as I can only imagine the devastation that he was seeing around him. One by one, he called me to tell me that each and every one was okay. Then he would tell me where he was headed next, "I am heading to Maw Maw and Paw Paw's. Call you when I get there. I love you, Mah!"

Destruction of homes on a street in Ocean Springs, Mississippi

The stories of what each of them endured as they stayed during the storm to only find themselves fighting for their lives. Finally the last call came in, it was from my brother Chris. He called to tell me that he, Tim and his daughters, Natalie and Cortney were all alive. However, he had lost everything. His car was in a tree and his house was completely gone, but they were all alive and that was all that mattered!

Those days were like no other. I think the hardest part was the waiting, not knowing if my family was okay or not. I had forgotten that feeling until the night we got the call from Nobile, the horrible feeling of waiting to hear if Blake was okay or not. The emptiness when the call finally came that the Coast Guard called off the search for him. The last call from Dustin, "Mah, what do you want us to do?" The decision I had to make to call off the search…the words I said back to Dustin, I will never forget, "Come home, baby…come home. Blake does not want to be found. Come home."

Tragedies such as Hurricane Katrina or losing someone in your life are life changing events. We seem to use them as time-markers in our lives…prior to Katrina or after Katrina. Prior to Blake's accident or after his accident. Time just stands still. The loss is so powerful that we struggle to regain some sanity or normalcy again. I can remember so many people told me that life would be different now and that I would need to start building new traditions and new memories. How do you change traditional events such as Christmas, New Years and Birthdays? It's not easy.

As close as we were as a family, building new memories have been so difficult as well as changing traditions that we built our lives making. This is our third Christmas without Blake and I can only say that the tears and pain still keep coming. Someone said to me that they thought the loss of Blake would be easier by now. "Easier," I thought? No. There is not a day that goes by that it becomes easier after losing a child or that special someone in your life. The only thing that helps me get through these days is God's Grace.

I trust that he has Blake in his care and Blake is doing his work by helping others more now than he could ever do here on earth. I trust Blake is still going to each of our families and friends checking on them one by one. I know that if he could communicate with me, he would or he will find a way.

And, I hear his voice over and over in my head, "I love you, Mom!"

"I was pushed hard, so that I was falling, but the Lord helped me. The Lord is my strength and my song; he has become my salvation." Psalms 118:13-14

Chapter 17

College Boys Clean Up

By Allen (Jr.) Gautreaux, Jr.

College Boys Clean Up was a collaboration of two masterminds, as you know Blake, Dustin and I rode out the storm by Mr. Tony's house in Beaumont. So while Katrina was hitting the gulf coast, we were surfing on Galveston beach. Great day of surfing! The following day, we were watching the news and began to hear of the devastation the storm had caused. Not being able to contact anyone at home because of all phone service being down, Blake and I immediately sprang into action. We took two 55 gallon barrels from Mr. Tony, filled them with gasoline, then went to local supply story and bought two chainsaws and water. We made our way back home stopping in Lockport first to check on everyone. Our hometown was fine, so then we left for Biloxi. We had to take Hwy 55 north to go around the damage through NOLA and Slidell. We made it to Ocean Springs and set up camp at Grandmas. Her yard was a wreck! We took care of family first. Mainly just clearing out yards of all debris and borrowing a trailer from a friend to haul it away.

Then family began asking us to help this person, then that person... After about a week of doing close to free labor and eating MRE's throughout the day, we thought we'd give ourselves a name and start getting paid for our services. By this time people were starting to receive their insurance money and we saw the opportunity to make some money. The name "College Boys Clean Up" was sparked as we were sparking a bowl to end our hard day's work. We laughed and thought it would be a catchy business name. So we went to Uncle

Henry's house and made about a dozen signs out of plywood, spray painted the name with both our numbers on it, and went stick them at every busy intersection across town. It took a couple of days, but the phone calls started pouring in. We answered very few callers on their first try. We'd just let them leave a voicemail, call them back at the end of the day, set up an appointment to meet at their home, assess the damages and provide them with an estimate. This went great for a few weeks. Profiting close to $500/day each.

Unfortunately we acted more like college kids than actual business men. And only being two of us with one truck, we could not keep up with all the calls. So we eventually stopped returning phone calls, and ended up making our way back home where things were back to normal at this time. The phone calls continued to pour in well into the following month after leaving Biloxi. I'd say the name was definitely a big hit!

Not very long after, my brother-in-law Chris calls me with an offer to help set up the FEMA trailers throughout New Orleans. The offer he presented was something I couldn't pass up. I began working for a local contractor and had Blake hired on the same day as me. We started as laborers first making $14/hr working 7days a week, up to 90-100 hours per week. The work was not hard at all. The hardest part was waking up every damn morning at 4am to make it to the shop in Kenner for 5am.

Our entire day was really drive time. NOLA was still being a complete ghost town, as there were no traffic lights working and no street signs to navigate your way around to find the house you were looking for. If we blocked 4 or 5 trailers in day, that was more than enough to make the bosses happy. Our day to day work habits is a whole 'nother story in itself...

I soon moved up to a foreman's position and had Blake as my "helper." This was the best and worst thing at the same time. It was great because now it's just us two on our own together, working at our own pace. Catching up on much needed sleep throughout the day and taking extended lunch breaks. But it was the worst when it came time to actually get things done. It's easy to tell your best friend to "go screw yourself" when you don't feel like doing any work that day, and Blake took full advantage of this. I actually got so pissed at Blake one day that I fired him in the morning, but by lunch time we were working together again.

Blake and Jr.

*"Work like you don't need money,
love like you've never been hurt,
and dance like no one's watching."*
—*Unknown Author*

Chapter 18

The Spirit of the People

By Blake Terry

New Orleans, Louisiana was once a city known for its unique heritage and stylish culture. It had many tourist attractions from the uptown bars to the down town French Quarter. The "big easy", a nick name given to New Orleans years ago, has a reputation for throwing the biggest hurricane parties. Almost every year we have had a few close calls during hurricane season, but it had been a long time since the city has seen a storm cause severe damage. The weather channel had issued hurricane warnings for south Louisiana and Mississippi, but little did everyone know what mother nature was about to show them.

The city's core of engineers built this city in the middle of a marshland area. The best way to describe the land the city was built on would be to call it a giant bowl. The city has levees that were built around it to keep the water out since most of New Orleans is below sea level. These levees were designed to with stand a direct hit from a category three hurricane. Along with the design of the levees, the dams and drainage of the city was designed under the same specifications to operate properly up to the conditions of a category three storm.

When Katrina laid her course, she changed the mentality of the designers who built the city. They were taught a hard lesson because the levees didn't hold up the way they were supposed to. This caused the engineers to start to go back and double check everything on the design that might have been overlooked. The engineering of the entire city failed because the drainage all works together with dams, ditches and levees. Once the levees broke they caused the city to fill up with water and the devastation of Hurricane Katrina began.

Once the rain and wind passed over and the sun came out, everyone who survived the storm saw firsthand as to what Mother Nature was capable of. The rebuilding process had begun. Neighbors that before only knew the family next door were working together with everyone from their neighborhood. I saw this first hand because I worked all over New Orleans setting up sight homes for these people. I can remember the look on their faces as we pulled up to cement slabs, all that was left of their homes. We were heroes to them. They had become humble and caring. People, who had lived next to each other for years and not spoke one word to one another, were sharing food and supplies to help themselves survive.

Before the water level descended, boat rescues had taken place. People who were enemies were riding in the same boat seeking safety. It was amazing to see these people, who were once enemies, come together to bring back their old city.

Before the storm hit New Orleans, the economy was doing great. Businesses were booming because the summer months always attracted tourists. Hotels, along with convention centers were steadily booked because people from all over were coming to see what New Orleans culture was all about. The oil field has brought many shipyards throughout the city. These shipyards were steadily building and repairing vessels because of the oil fields demand. The storm destroyed most of these facilities. All of the tourist attractions had been severely damaged from the flood. Small and large businesses saw revenue drops never seen before. The oil field lost millions of dollars because their shipyards and rigs had been damaged. The storm caused many businesses to struggle for many months. The total money lost was so high that the government couldn't provide the funds necessary for some of these businesses to rebuild. The unemployment rate was at an all-time high.

It has now been over a year since Hurricane Katrina destroyed New Orleans. The storm has taught us it will take many years for the structure of the city to be rebuilt, but the culture, heritage, and the spirit of the people will never be taken away.

"Restore to me the joy of thy salvation, and uphold me with a willing spirit." Psalms 51:12

Chapter 19

MIBAD

By Cindie Roussel

MIBAD stands for Minister, Insurance Agent, Banker, Attorney and Doctor. I taught Blake early on that these would be the most important people in his life if I could not be there to help him. I told him when you screw up, you need to have a personal relationship with each to be able to pick-up the phone and call them at any time. Blake did just that. He may not have gone to Church every Sunday, but he believed in God and Jesus. He believed in prayer and he believed in eternal life. I don't know if it was because I toted them all to Church every Sunday or if it was maybe the vision he had as a younger child. I just know that he believed and he was not afraid to share his beliefs.

When I married Tony back in 1983, we were married in a Catholic Church. The priest was not happy about marrying us with me already being pregnant and I was a Presbyterian to boot. He married us anyways. I think Grandma Terry had such an influence over the Church, they weren't going to mess with her. She wanted a Catholic wedding and by all means, we were going to have one!

As part of our wedding vows to God, I agreed to raise our children Catholic. By doing so, I exposed them to both religions, Presbyterian and Catholic. They came to church at the Raceland Presbyterian Church on Sunday's with me and they attended Catholic religion classes at Holy Savior in Lockport. Glenda Keegan has been the minister at Raceland Presbyterian Church for several years now. She is one of my closest friends and she knew my struggles in raising Blake. She knew his love of danger and adventure.

On Sundays when we would pray for those who were suffering or in need she would always add Blake to our prayers. She would say, "Lord, please protect Blake. We know he loves you and please keep a watch over him as he heads out into the Gulf." I always felt okay with him leaving out as I knew God was watching over him no matter where or what he was doing. Glenda was with me when Blake died. I can remember her words were so comforting but I know she ached in her heart as she has a son too.

When Blake started driving, he became close friends with our insurance agent, Pat Barker. In the first year of driving, Blake got six tickets, one was when he flipped the Tank pulling an overloaded trailer with Randy Boudreaux. When he got into trouble over mud running the jeep in the back of Gheens, it was Pat to the rescue. It was when Blake got his DUI that I was unsure if I would lose our insurance at that point, but Pat always came through. He knew Blake and he took care of him. I saw Pat a few months after Blake's death at a local restaurant and he came up to me with tears in his eyes. He told me that Blake and he were very close friends. I really did not know this as I just thought he only talked with Pat when he needed his help. He said that he had a nickname, "Scrap." However, Blake changed it to be "Scrap Iron." I laughed as he seemed to always have a nickname for everyone. It was his way of making you special to him.

I opened my bank account with Community Bank back in 1991 when I moved to Lockport. I met the Bank Manager there at the time, Ms. Emily Boudreaux. She was an average height woman with salt and pepper hair. She was so helpful whenever I needed anything that I insisted that each of my children open a bank account there once they started their first jobs. Blake learned how to manage money at a young age.

Uncle Bradley, my brother-n-law made a big impression on Blake. He taught Blake the value of money and how important it was to save his money. We all use to laugh and tell Blake that he was just like Uncle Bradley because Blake would borrow Scott's last five dollars for breakfast as he pulled a money clip of twenties out of his pocket to put the five on top of his twenties. He was tight and he loved his money.

He learned early how to borrow and pay back when he needed money. I could remember telling Emily to stop giving him loans and she would always tell me, "But Cindie, he is so handsome and I know YOU are good for it." She was so right, though. If he got into a pinch, he would call me to make sure he would not lose any kind of credit with the bank. Emily took care of him and he had built that relationship with her to make sure he could be trusted in paying back any money he borrowed.

When it came time to open his business, Emily was there. She setup all his finances and she made sure he had the best interest on his accounts. The one thing Emily said she loved about Blake was that he gave the best hugs! Emily is retired now and Rhonda Folse took Emily's position at the bank. Blake continued working with Rhonda as he did with Emily. It was important to him to maintain his relationship with his finance advisors.

I can remember bringing Rachel to meet Rhonda after Blake had died. Rhonda looked at Rachel with tears in her eyes and said, "You do know that he wanted to take care of you, Rachel?" I could tell that Rachel was a bit surprised by her telling her that. Rachel replied, "I never met a man who talked about his banker as much as Blake did." Then we all laughed. I think Rachel was more moved at the fact that Blake talked about his relationship with Rachel with Rhonda and that she knew him on such a personal level. Blake was not just a customer, he was family.

Blake never really had an attorney until he got his DUI. He decided that he wanted to fight his DUI charges that he got in Thibodaux back in 2007. Someone had told him that if he fought the charges, he may win and not have any of it show-up on his record. He hired a local attorney in Thibodaux. When they went to court, the evidence was too overwhelming. The Thibodaux Police Department had everything on video. Blake had fallen asleep at the wheel at a stop light down town Thibodaux. Another car passing by called the police stating that there was a truck parked in the middle of the road. When the police arrived, they turned on the blue lights. Blake woke up and drove into the median and almost hit a tree. Fortunately, no one was hurt except Blake's pocket book and pride.

Dr. Mike Marcello was our family doctor. I brought the kids to see him whenever they twisted something playing ball or when I needed him to drug test Blake every two weeks so that he could play ball! When Blake got older, I started letting him see Dr. Mike by himself as I wanted him to have a doctor that he could confide in. I knew that Blake had seen Dr. Mike for a number of times because he wanted to ensure he was not having any issues from diving such as the bends.

Bends or the proper term, Decompression Sickness, can be caused if a diver surfaces too fast, the excess nitrogen in the body will come out rapidly as gas bubbles. This can cause damage to several organs over time. When Blake died, I was undergoing tests for my heart and I had an appointment with my NP, Jo Foret who works in the same building with Dr. Mike. It was only a week since his memorial service and I can remember sitting in a room talking with several of the nurses and Jo when Dr. Mike walked in the door.

Everyone got up and left and he sat down next to me. He was off that day and he was in his normal every day clothes. Someone in the office called him to tell him that I was there. He said that he was so sorry to hear about Blake and that he needed to tell me something. He said that Blake taught his son, little Mike how to dive. He said, "The night Blake went down, my wife and I sat at the table thinking what if that had been little Mike? Who would we call? What would we do?"

He continued, "I guess we would call you." I was stunned as I had never once thought about someone else going through what I just went through. I never considered at that point that this could actually happen again. What would anyone do? It was at that very moment I realized that I needed to help someone else. I went home that evening and wrote *Burning Daylight*.

We created this book to be the life line help to families like Dr. Mike who have nowhere to turn. I was blessed that Blake had friends with the resources to try to find him, but I remembered sitting there helpless. Who do you call, 911? No, they could not help me. I needed a team of people who knew the water and the depths that Blake was at. I needed a team of people who knew the dangers and the risks involved. I needed a team to be there for me because every second, minute, hour was an eternity of pain waiting to hear if he had been found, dead or alive, at that point, you don't care, you just want him found. From there, we built the Blake Terry Memorial Foundation (BTMF).

The people not included in the MIBAD group but were just as important to Blake was his dentist and his hair dresser. Blake was known for that big beautiful smile and Dr. Rhonda Lorraine was the one behind making that smile so beautiful. Blake loved his teeth and he visited Rhonda faithfully. One day during his visit to Rhonda, he told her that he was in so much pain with his thumb as he had dropped a motor on his thumb and there was a blood pocket putting pressure on his finger. Blake had endured pain before, but Rhonda said he was in a lot of pain. He went to the emergency room and they had wrapped it and they told him to take Tylenol for pain. Fortunately for Blake, he had a dentist appointment the very next day. Rhonda took his thumb and drilled his thumb nail until the blood came bursting out and the pressure was relieved. Blake was no longer in pain and told Rhonda, "Do you know how much money you could have saved me?" That was Uncle Bradley coming out in him!

I went to see Rhonda a few weeks ago and she told me she thought she had lost a bracelet that I had given her. The power boat association Blake raced with had organized a memorial on the water in honor of Blake not long after his death. They had shirts made and they gave us these beautiful blue bracelets. These bracelets had Blake's race boat #3 with the quote, "Captain BT #3 laissez les bon temp rouler." This is a Cajun expression that means, "Let the good times roll." Rhonda said she was remodeling an old house when things were just not going right. She was down and frustrated with everything when she looked over at a pile of trash that the builders had stacked on the side of the house. She said she could see this blue thing sticking out of the pile of rubble. It was her bracelet that she had lost. She had no idea how it got there as she did not remember wearing to the house. She looked down at Captain BTs name and read the phrase. She said at that moment, her frustration was lifted and she smiled.

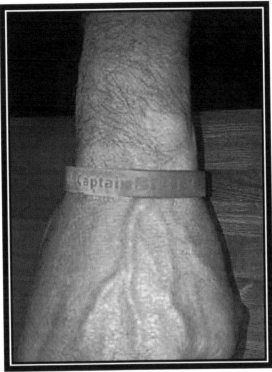

Captain BT# 3
"Laissez les bon temp rouler"

Leslie Ordoyne, was one of the first people I met when I moved to Lockport. I came to her with short bleach blonde hair and a perm. I think she nearly died and thought no way could I ever fix this mess, but she did. Blake was seven when Leslie started cutting his hair. He would call her on his way down to Fourchon and she would always make time for him. She loved to hear his stories as he always had one.

I went to see Leslie the other day and I could see she seemed different. I thought, she must just be tired and I told her how I was writing Blake's book. I noticed as customers were walking in, she would stare with caution in her eyes. Then she said something about going to the shooting range that evening. I said, "Leslie, you know how to shoot a gun?" She said, "Of course I do, but I want to practice." She then showed me her pistol she had laid on her station. I thought why would she have brought a pistol to work? She then proceeded to tell me that she had been robbed a few days prior and that she was going to protect herself should it happen again.

The look on her face and the fear and shock were so vivid to me. I know that the day Blake died, I felt robbed.
I am sure Rachel felt robbed, losing the love of her life and the soon-to-be father of Hank. I am sure Dustin and Whitney felt robbed losing their brother. I am sure all of Blake's friends felt robbed losing their best friend.

Here Leslie was taking action to prepare as she had her wake-up call. She was not going to be robbed again. The Bible says that we should always be prepared for our time as it can come to us like a thief in the night.

Blake was prepared. He had left no bad feelings behind or any resentment with anyone. He cared about you and he made sure you knew he cared. He built these relationships with each member of the MIBAD team so that when he did screw-up, he had each to turn to for help. He protected himself and he was prepared for what God had planned for him. I am sure the MIBAD team had no clue they were part of Blake's support group until now, but I can only say that

I am forever grateful to each of them for their help. They cared so much about my son and most importantly, he cared about them.

Blake

"The second is this, 'You shall love your neighbor as yourself.' There is no other commandment greater than these." Mark 12:31

Chapter 20

Paintball or New Orleans

By Nicholas Toups (Ponce)

The night began like a typical Saturday night. The pre-game drinking had already begun at Joose's house. The only significant difference was the two friends we had in town from Oklahoma. The two girls were old friends that came to town for a little vacation and a little partying. Little did they know; the party was going to be over before it even had a chance to begin.

Somehow, Blake got a hold of a paint ball gun. I don't who the gun was for, and I don't know how it ended up in Blake's possession. But nevertheless, Blake had a paintball gun and he wasn't afraid to use it. As the pre-game drinking continued at Joose's parent's house, Blake decided he wanted to bring the gun to New Orleans with us for the night. His reason for bringing the gun was to, "shoot road signs on the side of the interstate while hanging out of the window of the truck." I was actually for the idea. It sounded pretty damn fun if you ask me.

Joose, on the other hand, did not share Blake's enthusiasm. Joose was trying to keep the night relatively low-key and avoid any potential trouble with ole Johnny Law. This was simply not an option for Blake. He already had the notion in his head of bringing the gun and once Blake had an idea in his head there's pretty much no stopping him from following through.

After a relatively small argument at the Lagarde residence we decided it was time to leave. Blake told Joose that he would not bring the gun along for the trip, only after he looked at me with that big smile and tiny wink. Blake snuck the gun into the truck as we all piled in to embark on our journey to the "Big Easy." We traveled exactly one and a half blocks away from the house before Joose becomes aware of the gun onboard. He slams on the brakes and puts his truck in park, in the middle of the road. He immediately orders Blake to get out of the truck and bring the gun back to the house.

Anyone who knows Blake knows he is not one prone to taking orders. And anyone who knows Joose can tell you, he is not one to avoid confrontation. The two argued back and forth until Blake agreed to take the gun back to the house. We all get out of the truck in order to let Blake out of the back seat with the gun.

Upon exiting the truck, the argument begins again between the two of them. I cannot recall all of the details of the argument but I can tell you this; at one point, Joose took his shirt off and tossed it on the ground in preparation for a physical altercation. This was about the point where Jr. grabs his video camera and begins capturing footage of this potential heavy-weight bout.

Eventually, cooler heads prevailed and we defused the fight, or so we thought. As we were about to re-board the truck and continue on our journey to New Orleans, Blake notices Joose's shirt still laying on road. Blake walks by the shirt and casually moves it from his path with his foot. As Joose witnesses this act, the fury inside of him boils over and he screams, "You kicked my shirt?!" That's when the fighting commenced.

The fists began to fly as the two fought to display dominance over each other. The brawl lasted about a minute before the two eventually ended up grappling in some random person's front lawn. As they wrestled to subdue each other, Jr. continues to video tape the event. Joose finally gets Blake in to a head-lock and given the size of Blake's head, this is no small feat.

Blake would tell you that he had dental work earlier that day and his reason for stopping the fight was because he did not want to damage his teeth. The truth is, Blake probably underestimated Joose's wrestling skills and allowed him to get a pretty good hold on him.

After Blake verbally agrees to stop fighting, Joose releases his grip from around Blake's neck. Before the two can even stand up, the good ole Lafourche Parish police roll up on the scene. As they begin to hand cuff Joose and Blake for disturbing the peace, another officer arrives that personally knows Blake. The two are let go with a warning, I think. It all becomes hazy at this point because I was trying not to go to jail myself. The cops were getting a little cuff-happy at this point. The police finally let us leave so we hauled ass.

We never made it to New Orleans. After the incident we decided it would be best to go back to Blake and Tre's apartment in Thibodaux and play a little drunken candyland. We played, drank, got drunk and all passed out instead of spending the night in New Orleans. All because of a paint ball gun.

Blake and Jesse (Joose)

Chapter 21

Team Skanktuary

By Cindie Roussel and Thomas (Deke) Brown

The Skanktuary is a 21 foot fiberglass boat that was rebuilt by Blake and Nobile.

Blake and Deke boarding the Skanktuary

Blake put his blood and sweat into this boat as he loved her. As the weeks had passed after Blake's death, several had called me to ask me what I was going to do about the Skank? I can remember thinking, I really have no idea what to do with Blake's things, but I did know for sure, I would never get rid of the Skank.

The phrase, "Team Skanktuary" was discovered sometime back in Blake's college days. I had heard so many stories as to who was with Blake when the phrase was discovered that some of Blake's friends started to get upset with each other. It became an argument amongst his friends. So I went on a mission to find out the truth about the name.

What I learned was that Blake did not discover the "Team Skanktuary" at all. It was one of Blake's good friends from college. Blake named the boat "Skanktuary" back in high school, but the phrase "Team Skanktuary" was discovered later in college. The boat's name "Skanktuary" came from the movie, "The Ladies Man."

Leon Phelps played by Tim Meadows during the 1990s. The sketch was that of a broadcast program in which Phelps, a young, suave black man, would give dubious romantic advice and lovemaking tips. The Ladies Man openly proclaimed that he would court any woman at all, including skanks, providing the woman weighs no more than 250 pounds.

I could only imagine Blake introducing his boat like Leon Phelps did in the movie:

> *"My name is Blake Terry, my friends call me BT. I am an expert in the ways of love. I have made love to many fine ladies, from the lowliest skank, to the classiest, most sophisticated, educated, debutante, high-society, skank. So this is my fabulous boat. Or as I like to call it, my personal skanktuary... because this is where the magic happens."*

Here is the story behind the name - "Team Skanktuary"

By Thomas (Deke) Brown

When I first saw the boat I had never heard of the name and asked Blake what his meaning of it was supposed to be and he gave me that squinted eyed grin and said "It's a safe haven where skanks can roam freely." Naturally, I laughed.

Jared, Blake, Nobile, Primetime and Deke with their winning gar fish

On to the Team, I had made the mistake of telling Nobile we had some big gar (I had shot a 86lber) at the Ranch. Nobile kept on and kept on, and even though. I told him it wasn't going to work, we decided to make the fishing trip happen. We didn't even take the Skank, it was the Blue Torpedo. We launched my boat and the Blue Torpedo and then the Blue Torpedo wouldn't crank. There was too many people to fit in my boat, so we paraded out to the marsh with

117

my boat pulling the Blue Torpedo to go fishing. Dragging a broken down boat OUT to go fishing??? So long story short we ran out of beer and Jake shot one gar the size of my arm. I think we got back around 3 in the morning. In our drunken stupor, it was hilarious to take the picture with the one Little Gar. That night was named "Deke's Gar Hole Trip" and that's exactly what it was, a rotten gar hole. The crew consisted of Blake, Jared, Nobile, Primetime, Jake, and myself. I had gathered everyone up for the picture. Nobody was co-operating. Everyone was laughing at something Primetime had said, and at what I had said when I was taking the picture. That was a hell of a Team Skank trip.

When I got the picture developed I gave it to Blake and we both laughed. I referred to all of the idiots in it as "Team Skank." He said "Yeh, Team Skanktuary." That Christmas I got the stickers made for his Chrismas gift. He had no idea. I kept one for me and one for Jake, and gave the rest to Blake to hand out. He thought it was great. So I'm not going to say it was created in the hallway at college when I gave Blake the picture, but I think it was. If not, then it definitely was when he handed out the stickers to friends in Thibodaux and Lockport.

The famous "Team Skanktuary" sticker

Chapter 22

Who Needs a Steering Wheel

By Jesse (Joose) Lagarde

BT and I worked on the Skank on a Saturday morning to put in hydraulic steering. We finished up and talked to one of our buddies who said they were having a party at the Cajun Bahamas for the day; this is a sandy bottom in Dularge where everyone goes to hang out.

Blake (BT) and Joose

We launched in Lockport because we would rather ride in the boat then car and it takes a little less time and there are a little less cops on the water. We were well on our way and I was driving. BT looks

119

over and said, "Hey man, you forgot to put the nut back on the steering wheel." About 10 minutes past and I forgot about it. We came up to two boats going the opposite direction when he tells me to split the middle. I decide that there wasn't enough room and to go around instead. Well when I came back across the wake the steering wheel came off. We are heading straight toward the side of the bridge. We both tried to get the steering wheel back on and right before we hit, BT managed to turn the boat enough that the hit was not so bad. But it was bad enough to knock a hole in the side of the Skank. After we got the steering wheel back on, we determined that the hole was not bad enough to turn around so we continued on our way to Cajun Bahamas. Needless to say we somehow made it back safe!

Chapter 23

Salvaging the Skanktuary

By Ross Armstrong and Jared Uhlich

Ross - At this time in our lives, the only thing on our minds was diving, especially Blake! Fresh out of diving school and a vessel named the Skanktuary, we were ready for the water.

I arrived at Blake's house to meet him before the sun comes up and we ride to the back of the street to pick up Jared. Jared was the seasoned diver amongst all of us and he had all the gear we dreamt about. The weekend before Blake, Lynn (a girlfriend of Blake's at that time) and I dove out of Venice where Lynn's camp was located. It was a brutal trip, supposedly blue water is much closer from the beach in Venice. We never made it that far because it was too rough. After spending the day getting harassed by sharks we headed in with barely any fish at all. We got the hell beat out of us by rough seas and little did we know the Skank took much of a beating as well. Such a beating that one side of the windshield fell off. That wasn't enough to stop us. We loaded the Skank up and headed back home with the next weekend in our sights, Fourchon here we come.

Blake, Lynn, Jared and I headed for green water, bouncing shelf platforms trying to spear whatever we could. We hit a couple of platforms and had either no luck or sharks were lurking. Jared would jump out as we arrived at each platform to check it out before we wasted too much time mobilizing to find nothing at all. Not long into the trip we arrived at this one particular platform and struck gold, lots of snapper and no sharks to fight with yet. The plan is two divers in the water at a time and the other two stay in the boat. The two in the boat pull the fish off the guns and cock them for the next run so the diver didn't have to expense time and energy in the water doing so. Then we would swap out. We thought we were about to rack up. It's an intense moment of joy, the one we had been waiting on! So with Jared and Blake in the water Lynn and myself in the boat they come up quickly with two fish. We put the fish in the chest, re-rig their guns and they're off after another catch. In the midst of getting ready for them to come up with another run of fish we notice our feet were pretty wet. "No big deal" we thought, after all we are in a boat and I'm sure it was from reaching over the side just a second ago when we were taking the fish off. We go back to doing what we were doing then we notice random items that were in the hull were now sloshing around. Like flip flops and a few other items. I kid you not….this happened so fast it was not even funny. So we turn back to get a glimpse of the stern of the boat and that's when we knew we were going down. Within 45 seconds or so the engine was under water, so Lynn and I gathered everything that was valuable to us, fresh water we knew we would need for sure and with Blake hollering from the gulf, "GET THE SPEAR GUNS" we grabbed them too. ABANDON SHIP!

Jared - I wish I could remember the day or even the month for the matter, but it escapes me. I do recall it was sort of a nasty morning with the wind blowing harder than we had hoped for. This trip was made with four of us on board: BT, Ross Armstrong, Lynn and I. We originally planned to run about 60 miles WSW to the SS block to hunt, but the weather being what it was when we reached the launch, made us reconsider.

Instead, we decided to fish our old stomping grounds, West South Timbalier block. We loaded up and pushed off from the dock in BT's old 21' Chris Craft Scorpion - A.K.A. "The Skanktuary" with its big Evinrude FICHT engine. We had plenty of ice chests and diving equipment to go around, not to mention at least a 6 man supply of beer. All in all, a pretty standard load for a day of fishing. After a 15 mile run we shouldered up to our first rig in the ST-30 block and threw the hook.

After a few dives in low visibility water, we knew it was time to move on. The next rig we moved to was ST-37 (India) or just ST-37 (I). This was a relatively new platform with fresh paint. BT had the wheel and I had the rig hook. The current was in our favor and we were able to hook onto the dolphin of the rig with no problem. BT and I quickly got over the side and started shooting on the first dive. Lynn stayed on the boat alone. Time passes quickly when your hunting, so I'm not sure how long we were there but it surely couldn't have been more than an hour. I came to the surface with a mangrove snapper on my spear.

Once I pulled the fish up to me and had it at the gills, I turned for the boat. What I saw next was the Skank with her bow pointing up around 45 degrees and the rig hook about to straighten out on the platform. Ross and Lynn were hanging on to the helm and windshield to keep from being washed away with the rest of our belongings that had already been taken in the current and were forming a bread crumb trail of ice chests and cans from the stern.

About then BT surfaced and both of us hollered at Ross and Lynn to make a swim for it and join us at the platform. They got in the water right as the boat started to sink out of sight. The rig hook was going to go, so while BT grabbed Lynn, I swam into the cabin and tied it off long to the plus 10 level and watched as the rig hook gave way and the Skank vanished. Luck was at our side though, the ladder to the dolphin was still in place and usable which is no small miracle in the gulf. Without it, this would have been a very different story.

Jared Uhlich

We abandoned our fins and guns with fish still attached at the landing and began to climb. We were all bare foot and it was a relief to reach the smoke deck.

The platform was unmanned but in full operation, complete with a dog house or operations shack. We knew we needed to get inside and check for a radio or some kind of communication, but the door was locked. I was able to get the blade of my dive knife against the dead bolt and slid it just enough to open the door. Once inside, we looked around at all the gauges and control valves for a radio. No luck.

Then we found that there was a red telephone with a list of numbers. I picked it up and hit the code for "operations." A man answered and that was when we learned we were on a Chevron platform. I quickly relayed our situation to him to which he replied, "What do you want me to do about it?" Unbelievable! I told him I wanted him to call someone and get us out of there. He still didn't believe me and asked who I was and why I was bothering him.

Finally he realized this was really happening and he quickly dispatched two small Bell helicopters to collect us. I'm sure you can imagine the looks we got when we touched down at Leeville operations heliport and strolled through the terminal in wetsuits with spearguns over our shoulders.

BT bummed a cell phone from a man waiting for a flight and called Mr. Tony, Johnny Pinell and then Ms. Cindie. Johnny was at work but stopped what he was doing and headed to Fourchon to help us. We already had it in our heads to salvage the Skank with the water depth being only 60'.

After the story got around to all people who needed to know we set about planning the salvage in earnest. Dive gear was gathered, tanks jammed and a crew was assembled. Mr. Tony said that a boat could be pulled up with another boat if there was sufficient horse power available. No shortage there, Johnny's 36' Contender had 750hp at the time. At this point, all that was left to do was to return to the scene and explore the conditions of the wreck, so off we went, just a few hours after being flown in.

The Contender arrived at ST-37 (I) in no time and we hit the water. We found that the anchor rope had held and it was just long enough to allow the boat motor to rest on the bottom while the hull was maintained up right. This was perfect typical BT luck. In short order, a rope was tied to the U-bolt in the bow and a thorough inspection of the hull and her contents (or lack thereof) was made. It was then time to go.

Back on the Contender the anchor rope was cut loose from the rig and a strain was taken on the salvage line. With the camera rolling, Johnny eased the throttles forward and we all watched as the Skank broke the water's surface like a white whale. This was too easy, but sometimes things go your way I suppose. While under tow, BT and I jumped off the Contender with a couple of buckets and managed with some difficulty to get into the Skank while she was moving. The fear being that if we stopped she would once again sink.

Once inside we searched for damage and the cause of the sinking. She was a wreck, floor boards gone, windshield broken off, fuel tank broken from its bedding, you name it - it was damaged. We started bailing her out the rest of the way and soon we were all laughs and smiles as we rode back into port.

It was later found out that we had split the keel on a previous trip (maybe the weekend before) which was the cause of the leak initially. The real culprit was the bilge pump and the wiring to its float switch or really the missing wiring. When this was found out, I asked BT what he was thinking. He just laughed and said he would have gotten to it eventually and now was as good an excuse as any to fix it.

I always said Jesus walked with BT, because it was the only explanation to his good reckless fortune to me. Now I say it again, but this time there is no smile on my face. Fair winds and following seas my good friend. RIP BT.

Jared, Blake and Johnny

Blake and Johnny

Chapter 24

A Tattoo for an Arm

By Cindie Roussel

I was strict with the boys when they were young about not getting tattoos and body piercings. I just felt that these things were permanent and they would regret doing this later in life. It was something that I could at least stand firm on as a parent trying to teach my children discipline and respect. That did not last long as I finally gave into letting the boys color their hair. During ball season they both decided to color their hair blue. I thought the other parents were going to ban me from the ball games. I just figured, what is hair? They can cut it as soon as school started, and it gave them a chance to express themselves.

That all changed when Whitney asked if she could cut off all her hair and color it. I nearly died, but Scott reminded me that it was only hair. He was always keeping me balanced and he played fair between the kids whether I liked it or not.

Finally the inevitable happened. Blake hit the age that he finally stood firm and told me that he wanted to get a tattoo. I told him that the only way he could get a tattoo was that he had to remove it when he walked into the house. Something Scott's Dad, Art Roussel (Paw Paw Art) had told his brothers when they were younger. If you got a tattoo, you had to remove it or your body part before coming into the house. I thought that was pretty good compromise if you ask me.

Blake and I went back-n-forth over him getting a tattoo until he finally said, "Mah, I am moving into my apartment in Thibodaux, I really want your blessing before I get this tattoo." After pleading with me, I finally said yes. Of course, like most college kids, Blake moved back home after the first year of college, tattoo included.

Blake and Jr. went together to get their tattoos. Here is Jr.'s story:

We had been talking about getting a tattoo for a while but just wasn't sure on what we wanted. Sitting at The Palace (Scrubb and I's trailer at the time), my brother calls me and tells me that a fella in our subdivision is doing tattoos out of his house that night, if we wanted to go over. Now this guy had done all of my brother's tattoos so we trusted that he would do a good job at a great price. We leave the trailer and head to his house, which was actually his mom's house in the back of Nolan Toups. A 45 yr old Harley man giving tattoos out of his mother's garage should have been a red flag for us, but we went anyways.

We get there and he was all set up and ready for us. He immediately hands us a beer and asked, "Who's first?" Blake and I looked at each other skeptically, laughed, then I volunteered myself. As he was drawing the lines on my shoulders, he called his 80 year old mother outside to help even it out since I was going for a symmetrical tattoo. Another red flag, but we stayed anyways. Half way through my tattoo he stops to offer us another beer, then we see him pop a pill. This was the 3rd and very big red flag. I called my brother and he said not to worry about it. "He does his best work at the end of his night."

So I sit back down and let him finish. Unable to tell at the end because of the blood and swelling but the tattoo was all messed up. Lines weren't even connected and all different in thickness. So I'm done and its Blake's turn. He had the idea of the shark jaws, so this fella finds the closest thing that Blake's looking for and free hands it. Again, not looking so bad at the end, but he also had lines that didn't connect and just all around terrible work. We definitely got what we paid *for. I spent $100 and Blake spent $60... The following morning we laughed and realized how dumb we were. We immediately talked about going somewhere to get the tattoos touched up, elsewhere than the fella that lived with his mom in the back of Nolan Toups subdivision.*

Blake went to see Derek Matherne at Southern Sting and that's when they came up with the whole design of the shark behind the jaws. Jr.

Blake and His Shark Tattoo

When you lose someone in your life, as a part of the grieving process, they tell you to not do anything drastic. Don't sell your home or try to change your life too quickly. You need time to mourn and regain your thoughts. Well, I can only tell you that Scott and I wanted to sell everything. We were ready to buy a camp down in Fourchon and spend the rest of our days living on the water so that we could be closer to Blake. Nothing mattered anymore, work, bills, church, possessions, none of it mattered. I wanted to live on a secluded island and just be lost from society. I did not care anymore about anything except trying to find a way to get closer to Blake somehow. That's when it hit me, I need a tattoo. Yes, I need a TATTOO! So off I went to Southern Sting to meet with Derek Matherne. He was wonderful to me. He knew my pain and he was honored to do my tattoo. I told him that Blake would be in shock for what I was doing. Derek told me that Blake would be so proud of me for doing it. It took about four hours with my face buried in a towel crying, but I did it. Whitney and Tina Gravois, my assistant and close friend, held my hands as I cried and cried.

I can't imagine the pain Jesus must have felt when he was crucified. All I know is with every sharp pain from the needles digging in my back, I was letting my pain out. It was the most powerful experience I have ever had. I felt that this was the closest I would ever get to Blake again.

Well we did not sell our house or quit our jobs. We did not buy a camp in Fourchon or move to a secluded island, but I now have a tattoo of my beautiful son with an angel wrapped around him. I have a different relationship with Jesus as I have a better understanding of his suffering. His heart ached so much because he could not save us and he had to endure so much physical pain to save our souls. With every drop of blood that poured from my back was a mountain of tears pouring out of my heart from the hurt of losing Blake.

My Tattoo

*"Lord, all my longing is known to thee,
my sighing is not hidden from thee.
My heart throbs, my strength fails me;
and the light of my eyes- it also has
gone from me." Psalms 38:9-10*

Chapter 25

The Love of a Brother (the famous black-eye)

By Cindie Roussel

Blake and Dustin were always at it arguing about something. The two were so different it seemed. Blake believed the way you handled things was to go to blows. He thought if you take a few swings, it would break the ice and then you could sit down after and drink a beer together. Dustin on the other hand, was not one for confrontation. He believed in handling things in a more diplomatic manner. Discuss the issue and then if you don't see eye-to-eye, then at least you discussed it. Well that all changed when the hormones kicked in and both of them starting growing up.

Blake and Dustin

Blake would get a bit cocky with Dustin and he would continue to agitate him to see if he could get a rise out of him. Well one night it happened. Blake pushed Dustin too far. Blake dared Dustin to hit him and he DID! Dustin hit him so hard he knocked Blake to the ground and Dustin figured that was it, I'M DEAD! Blake got up, shook his head and walked away. The next day Dustin called me upset that he broke Blake's cheek. He said he heard something crack. Immediately, I called Blake. He was mad at Dustin. He said that Dustin punched the crap out of him and he did not know if anything was broken or not.

Then within a couple of days, something started to happen. Blake's eye became swollen and bruised. He had a black ring that a pair of sunglasses could not hide.

Blake's famous black eye

Blake's friends started giving him grief that his little brother had finally become a man. Dustin passed the final initiation to man-hood by giving his older brother a black-eye. The more everyone made over it, the prouder Blake became of his brother. He was so proud, he took a picture to keep. It was the ultimate achievement to Blake. Things were different between Dustin and Blake after that. Nothing could break the bond they had between each other. They had an understanding and from that day forward, they were closer than two brothers could ask for. There were no more issues between them.

I can remember Gary Jr., Rachel's brother told me a story about the first time Blake joined them on a family vacation. Gary Jr. and his brother Clayton were always at odds with each other. Blake told Clayton, "You got to settle this with Gary. You can't keep all that anger built up inside." Now Gary is laying in a lounge chair on the beach while Blake is talking to Clayton. He looked at Clayton and winked at him and said, "Come on!" They both took off running, grabbed Gary's chair and threw him into the water, chair and all! Gary came up swinging. That was it! The two of them let all of their anger out! Gary said, "Ms. Cindie, things were different between Clayton and me. Blake taught us that being brothers were important and that we need to not hold things back."

Maybe Blake was right, at the end of the day you just need to lay it all out there. Don't hold anything back; give it your best swing with all you got…what the hell do you have to lose? Then after it is all out there, there is nothing in your way to becoming the best you can possibly become.

Dustin and Blake (Brother's again)

Chapter 26

Team Terry Racing

By Cindie Roussel

Team Terry racing started back in 1985, when I decided to start racing with Tony. It was not something I would declare that I was great at, but none the less, I was racing. I had a 13 foot tri-hull with a 25 hp Johnson motor. I ran with a 15" prop but would change to a 17" prop for speed. I was every bit of 90 pounds soaking wet with a weight limit of no less than 600 pounds when you finished a race. I had pink flames running down the side of the boat with a pink helmet and a pink driver's suit. Down the side of my boat were the letters, "Pretty N' Pink." I was pretty sharp if you asked me.

We were part of the Biloxi Bunch Boat Racing Association back then with about 20 members. Blake tugged along with us and between boat races; he was hanging in the pits with Grandpa Chester or anyone else who would watch him while we were racing. I was racing my boat the summer of 1985, little did I know, I was pregnant with Dustin. (Hummm…maybe that is why he had it in his blood.)

When Tony and I divorced, I kept "Pretty N' Pink" and when we moved to Lockport, I sold her to a couple of boys down the bayou for $1500.00. I can remember Blake crying in his room when I sold her. I tried to explain to him that we needed the money and that I was never going to race again. I guess at that point, he was never going to let money stop him from doing what he loved. He loved being out there watching his Dad race and he wanted to be part of that life no matter whether I wanted it or not.

This all changed when Blake and Dustin tried to convince me to let Dustin join the racing team. My heart fell to my stomach when they both tried to convince me to let Dustin race. "Mah, Dad has a boat that he can let Dustin drive at the next race." Blake said. "I don't think so!" I replied. "But Mom, Dustin is pretty good with the boat and I think he was made to be a racer." Blake said. "WHAT? So your Dad let him race? Dustin has no business in a RACE BOAT!" I said, now I'm PISSED OFF! "Mom, I want to race."

"Dustin, you don't even know how to drive a boat, LET ALONE RACE ONE!" I snapped back. "Mah, that's because you baby him too much. He really knows what he is doing." Blake replied. "Did your Dad put you up to this?" I questioned, looking to blame someone for this crazy idea that my sweet little Dustin could not have come up with on his own. He was my baby and I was not about to let him do this.

"Mah, he's GOOD! You need to give him the chance." Blake said in a reassuring voice as though he knew that I would give in. "Well, I won't go to watch any of your races." I said, hoping this would discourage this whole crazy idea. They both grinned at each other and then hugged my neck. "Mah, I love you." Dustin said. Little did I know, Dustin was becoming the hottest little rookie in his class. He had racing in his blood and he was GOOD! I vetoed going to any of his races, but I would call Blake before and after every race to check up on Dustin. Blake eventually joined his brother and Dad racing and I did not stop him. I trusted Blake knew what he was doing as he had driven boats most of his life and he seemed to be cautious about safety. I did not like it mind you, but I let him go.

I thought all was okay with the world, and then the inevitable happened! WHITNEY GOT THE FEVER! I should have known. Whitney was always trying to be like "one of the boys!" I can remember living on Linda Circle and looking out in the back yard. All three had their pants down peeing on the fence. The only problem was Whitney was crying. The boys told her that she had been bad and that I had cut her "thing" off! She was so upset. She cried, "Mah, please put it back! I promise I will be good!"

Dustin and Blake started with the same approach by trying to smooth things over about how GREAT boat racing was and how SAFE it was …I knew something was up, but I never imagined what was about to happen!

"Mah, Whitney wants to race boats and she is really good!" Blake said. "She knows all about the boats and she has watched us and she knows what to do." Dustin said. "OVER MY DEAD BODY!" I shouted. "But Mom, she really wants to join us and Dad has a boat already built for her." Blake replied.

"I FORBID HER TO RACE!" as I threw a shoe across the room hoping to hit one of them. Dustin moved quickly behind the door as he felt the wind from my shoe. "But Mah, YOU DID IT and she wants to do it too!" Blake said sarcastically. "We will make sure she is okay. We won't let anything happen to her, we PROMISE!" Dustin said.

After yelling and screaming for a while, I began to cry. "Whitney, is this what you want?" I asked knowing that I was defeated. "More than anything, Mom!" Whitney replied. "You know, I won't come to any of your races," I repeated. Again, I was desperate hoping that this would discourage her from racing. "I understand, Mom. I love you!" as she wrapped her arms around me trying to reassure me that this was all okay. Team Terry Racing Team was now a TEAM!

I look back now and I am so grateful I let them do this one thing they all enjoyed together. Crazy as it seems, it was the one thing they shared and loved so much. Scott and I finally went to watch them race in Orange Texas the year before Blake died. It was exhilarating to watch the three of them on the water. They circled like sharks waiting to catch their prey. When the flag dropped, they got into formation and you could hear the engines roar as they race to the start line.

Blake, Dustin and Whitney
"Team Terry Racing"

Lap after lap we would holler and scream, "Go Team Terry!" as it did not matter who beat who, as long as one of them placed. So proud to be in the crowd watching the three of them, but yet scared to death that something might happen. Dustin with his boat flying in the air hitting the waves as Blake and Whitney were not far behind him. The crowd went crazy over the three of them. When it came time to sign autographs, the boys stood under the tent as the crowd swarmed Whitney. She was this little girl who any mother in her right mind would not allow to be in a race boat, but there she was. She had knocked a hole in the side of her boat the first heat, so they duct taped her boat for the second heat. She won! At the drivers booth, Dustin and Blake stood there waiting to sign autographs but no one came up to them for their autographs. Instead, they swarmed Whitney. They lined up to see this amazing little girl who beat both her brothers. Blake looked at Dustin and said, "Dude, I think we better go make sure she is alright."

Whitney, Dustin and Blake at the driver's signing

Chapter 27

Lubbock Texas

By Dustin Terry

Blake, Whitney, and I have so many stories. When it comes to racing, very few of the stories have something to do with the actual race. The majority of our trips were filled with the traveling, turning wrenches at my dad's, hanging out with our racing buddies, fighting with our competition, fighting with each other, and hoping to come home with a trophy and a hangover. Of all of our races, the one that we still tell at every race is one of our trip to Lubbock Texas. This race represents to me, what life is all about.

This race started out a little different than most. I had to work late into the week, so for the first time, I got to fly to the race site and skip out on the days of prep work and hauling. Had I have known then, what I know now, I wouldn't have taken the "Hollywood" route.

Whitney and Blake were taking my truck up there while towing one boat, and Dad and Racing Ray were driving the box van with two boats behind it. Whitney had been dating this new guy that Blake and I had met a couple times. We hadn't had a chance to really get to know him. He was from out of town and would come to Applebee's and sit at my bar. Whitney worked with me, and Blake ran up tabs at the bar and never paid. (Blake would always holler, "put her drink on my tab" and follow it up with a shit-eating grin.) We didn't know much about this guy, other than he was a big, corn-fed, hillbilly named Daniel that had a thing for Whitney. Never afraid to approach us and have a drink. He always walked in and acknowledged Blake and I before Whitney. This race, Whitney decided it was time to bring him. I don't know what happened on the 12 hours of driving to the race, but by the time that I had arrived, Daniel was 1/3 the way to being a part of Team Terry Racing. Blake was won over. Whitney had gotten really sick on the way up and was fighting to get on the course all weekend. Blake decided it would be funny to make Dad think that Whitney was experiencing morning sickness, and that's why she brought this new guy to the race. It was so believable because Daniel would never leave Whitney's side. He just wanted to help and Blake took advantage of it.

I flew into Dallas and was picked up by my friend, Aaron Autin. He had some family that went to Texas Tech and after a couple hours of driving, we arrived at their house in Lubbock. I had spoken with Whitney and arranged a time to meet them at the hotel. By the time they arrived Friday night, Blake and Daniel had wiped out the ice chest of beer. Blake wasn't driving for the last leg, so he had no clue as to where he was on a map. This would create a big problem for us the next night. We checked into the motel that had been suggested to us by John Schubert, the race director. It was called the "Welcome" Inn. If you are ever in Lubbock Texas, swing by the "Welcome" Inn, but do not stop, keep your windows up, and your doors locked. The team stopped in at the race site to drop off the boats and have a couple more beers with our racing buddies. Aaron and I hung out with our Red Raider friends until everyone arrived at the motel. We all checked in some time before 2 a.m. I know this because the motel shared a parking lot with a salsa club that had not closed yet. Once the doors shut, a huge fight broke out in the parking lot. All the racers seemed to find their way up to the second floor to watch the brawl. Whitney, Daniel, Blake, and I shared a room. Even if we wanted to sleep before 2 am, we didn't have a choice. Our room was directly over the "Welcome" Inn bar, the same bar that someone had been stabbed in 8 days before our arrival. Once it was time for bed, Blake did what he always did at a motel. He threw the top blanket of the bed onto the ground. I don't think anything disgusted him more that the unwashed linens of a motel, and him and I did our best to stay out of the sink hole in the middle of the mattress.

Saturday morning had arrived and it was time to go racing. I had new race shirts made for this race because this was the first season that all three of us were racing together. I had just gotten a new boat and Blake decided my old boat was going to be his own creation. He was the original driver for Whitney's #9, but after he made the decision to go on a fishing trip instead of a race, our dad gave in to Whitney's begging and gave her Blake's boat. (We never expected her to keep racing. We thought she would give it back after her first race.) My new boat was hauling ass, so it didn't help my "Hollywood" status for the weekend, and Blake had really did his homework on his new motor. He had learned how to set up the boat on illegal fuel and had our slowest boat and motor running at the front of the pack.

This weekend was full of races. We had 6 qualifying races on Saturday, 7 qualifiers on Sunday, and a long 20 lap final at the end of the weekend. Whitney fought her "morning sickness" and made it through every race. On Saturday she had good finishes, but not her normal. She would normally when a qualifier or two and had made it to the podium in finals before. The reason she couldn't win any races on Saturday is because Blake and I kept finishing 1st and 2nd. If I would win, he would get 2nd. If he would win, I would get 2nd. We couldn't believe it. This was Aaron and his friend's first race. They thought we did this at every race. Nobody else could compete with us for six races in a row.

As soon as the last qualifier on Saturday ended, Blake cracked open his first beer. No one was going to catch us on Sunday. Whitney and I had shared a podium with 1st and 3rd, but Team Terry never finished #1 and #2. We had been close so many times without this kind of speed. I walked around the pits talking with the other drivers, just fishing for a chance to gloat. Every driver we spoke with had something to say about how either Blake or I had wet them down at some point. I didn't have anything to drink. I planned on meeting up with Aaron and the Red Raiders later for drinks. Blake was just going to party in the pits. He had already begun to smoke cigars. We always saved them for Sunday after a victory. Most of the drivers were veterans and just laughed at our ignorance. So many of them had been there before, but one racer just couldn't keep away from talking smack with us. A rookie by the name of Wesley (Wes) Cheatham running the #4 boat. Wes was just like us, a child of a former boat racer. He was 20 years old and was ready to make his mark in racing. As the evening went on, Wes got tired of all the bragging coming from the Team Terry crew. I was ready to leave the pits and head out for my first beer when Wes looked at Blake and said, "I'll drink any of you Terry's under the table!" Blake looked at me and said, "Get the truck. We are going out." Blake gave Wes our room number at the "Welcome" Inn and told him to meet us and come see who will out-drink whom.

We got back to the room and Whit was puking in the toilet. Blake and I barged in the door and told them about this new kid and what he'd said. Whitney laughed and told Daniel to go out with us. Daniel decided to stay with Whit. He still regrets it today. We were sitting in the room having beers for a couple minutes. We figured he wouldn't show and were about to head out when a knock came at the door. Wes walked in with a pair of jeans and cowboy boots. He had ironed a crease in the leg of them. This is a trend in Texas that we were unaware of. We began to wonder if it was a good idea to bring this guy out, but before we could think twice, we were on the road.

I called Aaron to see where we could meet them, and he told me the restaurant that they were at was kind of fancy. I didn't think it was a good idea to join them yet because Blake had been drinking for a few hours. I wanted an environment that was more suitable for him to get some dinner before we went to the bar. Just so happened that a bar&grill was about a mile from my friends. Once we pulled into the parking lot, Wes revealed to us that he was underage. I was of age but I still had my fake ID from high school in my wallet. The ID was Blake's and Ross Armstrong's. The reason I say "and" is because the picture on the ID was of Blake but the information was a description of Ross. This was not a fake ID for Blake because when he was underage, he went to the DMV, stating that he was Ross Armstrong and had lost his ID. Only Blake could pull off something like that. So, I gave the ID to Wes and he threw it back at me saying, "This won't work. They are gonna know that it's Blake." Blake replied, "It'll work. You have to order the pitcher. When the girl comes to the table, have the ID up for her to see." Wes ordered the beer with so much confidence that she never even looked at it and asked for Blake and my ID. She told Wes that it was obvious he was over 21, but we were questionable.

We sat there for about two hours, ordering pitcher after pitcher with a couple shots thrown in. We had an order fried pickles that Wes destroyed and some wings to put something in our bellies other than alcohol. Aaron called and said they were ready to go to the bar, so we closed out and hopped in the truck.

At this point, I was feeling pretty good, Wes was rambling, and Blake was mumbling. It began to rain right as we got onto the road.

The roads were slick so I started to have fun with the truck, making it fishtail through slow intersections. As I was merging onto the highway and stomped on the gas to have some fun and the back end of the truck got out of control. I slide across four lanes of traffic and over corrected back across four lanes again. Somehow I saved it and we started cheering. Wes kept shouting, "Hell yeah, we are tri-hulls racers baby!!!" As soon as we thought we had just pushed our luck to the limit, Johnny Law popped up in my rear view mirror. Once I saw the lights flashing, I started cursing. Blake in his drunken haze just says, "Just move over. They are going to go around us." I shouted at Blake, "What?! We just slid across four lanes of traffic!!!" I pulled over to the right side of the road and immediately told Blake, "You gotta switch with me! I've already got one DUI on my record." Blake opened his eyes for the first time in hours to look at me to say, "Yeah, right!" I looked back and pleaded that I would bail him out, and he'd never had a DUI before. I had already jumped to the back seat with Wes when he finally said "Ok, give me my hat and toss me my shoes." I hopped into Blake's spot in the front and tossed him his hat. I reached down and tried to give him his flip flops when he said, "No, my shoes in the back!" We tossed those to the front just in time. The cop's flashlight burned into our eyes and was followed by the officers squeal.

Officer: "Who the hell wants to go to jail tonight?"
Blake: "What do you mean by that?"
Officer: "You guys just tried your best to wipe out everyone on this road. Now where are you coming from?"
Blake: "Louisiana, sir. We are here for the boat races."
Officer: "I didn't ask where you are from. Where are you coming from? Where are you headed?"

This is the point where it would have been helpful if Blake knew anything about how he got to Lubbock, where the motel was, or even what highway we were on at the time. We were on a highway heading south, the lake we raced on was north, the motel was west and Louisiana was east. The only response he could think of was:

"Louisiana, sir. We are here for the boat races."

It was all he knew and he stuck with it. I did my best to try and take the heat off of Blake.

Officer: "Where are ya'll coming from?"
Dustin: "I'm a driver, I was at a bar off 289 and called my crew chief to come pick me up."
Officer: "I'm not asking you. Have you had anything to drink, because I smell alcohol?"
Blake: "He just told you he was drinking. I'm just trying to get him back to the pits. We are from Louisiana, trying to race out here."

The officer told us to stay there and walked off in frustration. Blake never took his hands off of 10 & 2 and left his hat low. Meanwhile I'm trying to give Blake a crash course in where we are. Blake wasn't too worried because the officer wasn't in uniform. Then we all looked back and a second cop pulled in. That's when Wes started rambling, "There are gonna be three less tri-hull drivers in the morning." Blake and I kept working on a game plan, trying to get Blake to retain any information about where we were. Wes kept rambling until Blake finally turned around and told him, "Just shut up. We are getting out of this." Then, two cops approach the window and ask Blake to step out of the truck. That's when I knew it was over. Blake had been drinking for hours. There is no way anyone could believe he could even start the truck. The cops brought Blake to the back right side of the truck, so I could see them testing him the entire time. I had to keep telling Wes to keep quiet. All the windows were down, and he kept rambling about how drunk Blake was. I am ashamed to admit that I put my head down and began to pray, "God, if you will let us get away with this, I will take us straight home and straight to bed. I won't drink and drive ever again." I lifted my head and stared into the rear view mirror. Blake was standing on the down slope of a ditch in wet grass in the rain. The two cops were standing above him on the shoulder of the road. Both of them were waiting for him to slip. Blake later told me what he was doing during the eye test. The officer in uniform raised his finger with his flashlight in Blake's eyes and asked him to follow from side to side. Blake had his knees slightly bent and his hands clinched in a tight fist by his side. He looked like he was skiing down a mountain. He locked everything into place so all he had to do was focus on his eye movement. As the cop moved his finger to the right, Blake would slowly move his eyes down to the cops elbow. As he moved his finger to the left, Blake would focus on his left shoulder. They went back and forth until the cop asked Blake, "Are you sure you can see my finger?"

I watched this go on for what seemed like 30 minutes when I see Blake walking back to the truck. Blake sat down with the windows still open and whispered, "We're good." This was almost a huge mistake because Wes shouted with disbelief, "Are you serious?!" At that moment, Blake and I almost threw Wes out the truck. The cop out of uniform walked back up to the window, gave Blake his ID, and told him, "Get the hell out of here." Blake had them convinced that he was more blind than drunk. I asked Blake if he could drive us to the motel. He replied, "My work is done, and we are going to the bar!" He idled the truck down the shoulder to the next exit and put me back in the driver seat. We briefly debated kicking Wes out the truck for almost blowing it, but at this point, there was too much love in the truck.

We finally met Aaron and the Red Raiders at the bar. They couldn't believe the story that just happened. Blake and I were on a roll. We had our arms around each other's necks the rest of the night and kept shouting, "Get your guns up!" just to fit in with the locals. We ordered shots at the bar when Wes finally admitted defeat. We all downed them and started sharing our story with anyone that would listen. The three of us were next to each in a long urinal and noticed that someone had thrown up in it. We all laughed that someone couldn't handle their alcohol. We hit the dance floor for a couple songs until we noticed that Wes had fallen asleep sitting straight up in his barstool. Everyone in the bar got a picture with him. Blake and I met again in the bathroom, and Blake realized that whoever threw up must have had fried pickles. We laughed and headed back out to the dance floor. After another couple songs, Blake fell asleep sitting straight up in his chair. Every person that took a picture with Wes lined up for their photo with Blake. The next thing I remember is Whitney waking us up. She said we came in to the room, laid down, and spooned. The bed sunk in the middle and that's my story. We all headed down to my truck to find the doors wide open and the keys in the ignition. Nothing was stolen so we knew it was going to be another lucky day.

We stopped at the gas station to get some fuel and Blake went inside to get some breakfast. We were all gassed up when Whit says, "Look at this." Blake came walking out with bags full of food and drinks and a sweet new cowboy hat on his head. Then, Daniel comes out with his own and that's when he was 2/3 the way to being a part of Team Terry Racing. That was when he had won me over. I went in to get one for myself then we headed to the race site. On the way there, Whitney said that she had to play a song that reminded her of the night that Blake and I just had. She said, "I know ya'll hate country, but this is too perfect." She put on "Out Last Night" by Kenny Chesney. We pulled into the pits hanging out the truck with our cowboy hats shouting, "Get your guns up." We pulled up to Wes' trailer to find him laying down in the shade, just looking for any hangover relief. We all were.

Blake and Whitney

As Sunday went on, Blake was the first to go. As soon as we started the qualifying heats, Blake took out three turn buoys, dragging them across the course. Whitney didn't drink the night before, but we brought her down with us. She got slammed by another driver on the opening lap and floated outside the course. I was still qualifying well and was on the pole for the final. Blake had fallen back to 4th. Whitney was down to 6th. As final approached all three boats were getting worked on. Blake and I were no help. My dad was getting on us about going out and struggling to be able to race. That is when Daniel said what would define our team was all about. "If you're gonna be dumb, you gotta be tough." I think that is when he became 3/3 on being a member of Team Terry Racing.

Blake with a buoy hooked to his boat

We all loaded up and lined up for the final heat. I put my new cowboy hat in my boat so I could put it on for my victory lap. I told Blake I would try to open him a hole so we could get this 1st & 2nd. As the flag dropped, I came into turn one, and my battery came sliding into my lap. I fell from first to seventh in the first turn. Blake was pushed out wide and was all over the course until flipping his boat for the first time. Whitney moved up a spot and finished in 5th. We were able to strap down my battery while the rescue moved Blake's boat off the course. I got close to the front before the battery broke loose again. I finished in 3rd and the battery destroyed my cowboy hat that I was going to flaunt on my "victory" lap. Blake took out the fastest boat on the course and crashed it. If he hadn't crashed, I wouldn't have gotten my trophy. He even had to give me his cowboy hat to wear on the podium since I destroyed mine. We didn't care where we finished that day. We had won the night before and that third place trophy is my favorite to this day. Blake put it all on the line for me and he did what he always did best. He came through when he needed to. Racing with Blake and Whitney has been the greatest experience of my life.

Dustin takes Third Place

"Blake put it all on the line for me and he did what he always did best. He came through when he needed to."
Dustin Terry

Chapter 28

Ready to Fight, No Matter the Size

By Cindie Roussel and Jesse (Joose) Lagarde

There were many stories of the wild nights, women, drinking and bar room brawls that I heard about. I am sure there were just as many that I did not hear about as well. Blake considered a night a success as long as no one got hurt or thrown into jail. Blake worked as hard as he partied. Although he loved to have a good time, it amazed me how well disciplined he was with making sure he took care of his body. He believed in keeping in shape. I can remember that he was playing football in high school when he felt that the school workout program was not a very good one for building a strong and healthy body so he joined the gym. He finally told me that he was not going to play his senior year of football because he just was not built strong enough to play. I was so heartbroken but he was right. All of a sudden, he shot up tall and became slim. He was no longer stocky and he no longer had that thick chest that he had before. Next thing I knew, Ponce, Joose, Jr. and Boudreaux were working out. They were taking before and after pictures of themselves. Body building posters were hanging all over his room with Arnold Schwarzenegger poster of his famous poses. I guess Blake figured if he continued to play hard that he better be in shape for that one big fella that he would have to go up against.

The story that I have included in this chapter is the same story from Tyler Cheramie in Chapter "The Mouth Piece" but this is from Joose's version.

Blake body building

Funny, both Joose and Tyler did not know each other at the time but were the beginnings of friendships between the Fourchon boys and the Lockport boys.

We would always go to parties down the bayou. I remember one night this guy came up to BT and said, "Hey man, heard you was sleeping with my girlfriend." BT said, "No man, I don't know what you are talking about." BT could read through this guy and knew he was just looking to start a fight. BT turned to me and said, "Hold my beer" and then he swung back and punched this guy as hard as he could. Now this guy was 6'5" about 250lbs. This guy took BT's punch like it was nothing and started throwing BT around and then they both took out the DJ system. After it was all said and done, BT came out of it without a scratch, turned to me and said, "Can I have my beer back?" BT was never afraid to fight no matter the size of the guy. He believed in settling the issue and moving on.

Blake may not have won all his fights, but he was ready no matter what. He knew that he had to not only have his mind clear but he needed to physically be ready. In the Bible, Philippians 4:13, I can do all things through him who strengthens me. I believe Blake thought he could do anything if he set his mind to it. He took pride in his body and he believed in keeping in shape. 1 Corinthians 6:19, do you not know that your body is a temple of the Holy Spirit within you, whom you have from God? You are not your own. Through his death, both Scott and I stopped taking care of ourselves. I know that I cried every day for the entire year that I lost all my eyelashes. I drank at least three glasses a wine every evening and then I felt horrible the next day. None of it mattered. It was all I had to keep me sane. So many would tell me how well I have done to survive losing him. I really wasn't doing well but I could put on that fake face with a smile like everything was fine while inside I was so torn-up. We all find excuses to not take care of ourselves and I just did not care anymore. But as I started to see myself change, I could hear Blake telling me in my head, "Mah, you need to take care of yourself." I started gaining weight from the alcohol and my hair started to fall out along with my eyelashes. I had become that person that people were probably saying, "Did you see Cindie lately? She looks so bad since she lost her son." I did not want to be that person. Sometimes we try so hard to hang on to our faith but the devil can drive us into the dark world. I was living in this dark world. I missed Blake so much. We all have our tests of faith and I was being tested. Carla and Todd Dufrene, dear friends of mine, lost their son, Cody when the boys were all in school. Todd was the first to come to the house when Blake went missing. He put his arms around me and he told me, "Your faith will be tested. Don't give up on God. He is not giving up on you."

My heart ached so much and my body was wasting away. 2 Corinthians 4:16, we look not to the things that are seen but to the things that are unseen; for the things that are seen are transient, but the things that are unseen are eternal.

Blake doing his "Arnold Pose"

Chapter 29

Blake, My Man

By Cindie Roussel

In July 2006, Chad, Kathie's middle child, and his soon-to-be wife Tammy planned a destination wedding in St. Lucia. Kathie arranged the booking of our rooms and flights with their agency. We planned a year in advance so everyone could pay monthly and all expenses paid prior to flying out. We were so excited because our family had really never taken a vacation together and this seemed like it was going to be so much fun!

Blake, Aunt Happy and Whitney in St. Lucia

Blake and Whitney were not dating anyone at the time so we booked the flights and their rooms together as a couple. We figured that they could share a room and we could get the discounts by them sharing the expenses.

The day came that we had everything packed, everyone had their passports with money to spend. We were very excited as this was truly going to be our very first REAL vacation as a family.

When we landed in St. Lucia, we had to go through customs which I, of course was worried as I never knew what might happen with Blake. Everything checked out okay and then we all boarded onto a bus. We traveled up the mountain side and stopped at several little huts to buy the local island beer. Once we got to the top of the mountain, we pulled into this amazing resort. The view was just beautiful with the mountains and crystal blue water, it was like we were on top of the world.

We each got our room keys and headed to our rooms to get ready for a night of relaxation. Our rooms had two queen beds with glass sliding doors around the pool area. You could see the beach and ocean from each room. As we all gathered outside by the pool area to start our night of fun, it became clear to Blake that something was not right? It hit him, "This was a couple's resort." "COUPLE'S" mind you...there were no women to pick up as they were all married or were getting married. All of a sudden his world changed quickly and he had to think fast. Blake became good friends with the islanders.

Blake and Candace, his cousin

The next morning, outside the pool, everyone was having a great time and all you could hear from the bar was "Blake, My Man!" The cleaning ladies, the bar maids and the waitresses were all calling him by name, "Blake, my man!" He knew everyone in the place and he had learned the island pretty fast. By the time we were ready to head home, he was still hanging out with the islanders. Yes, he was missing when it came time to leave but fortunately, he showed up right before the bus pulled out.

I go back to that fun week and remember how beautiful St. Lucia's was and how we had the best time as a family, but most of all, I can still hear the islanders saying, "BLAKE, MY MAN!" Blake could have made the vacation miserable but instead he did as he always had done. He made the best of a bad situation.

*"When we are no longer able to
change a situation - we are
challenged to change ourselves."
Viktor E. Frankl*

Chapter 30

You Never Know Who Is Listening

By Cindie Roussel

Blake's senior year, he told me that he was not going to play football anymore. He had a serious look on his face as he was afraid I was going to be upset. He said that he was not big enough and the players were getting bigger each year. He really felt he was not college football material. I was fine with it as now was the time to really decide what he wanted to do in his life. He wanted to be a Naval Architectural and Marine Engineer but he was going to need a job while going to school and the sugar mill was just seasonal.

He loved working out at the local gym so he convinced the owner to let him have a job. He started working between classes helping out whatever they gave him to do. "This was the perfect job." I thought. Blake was a health nut about his food and he was self-conscious about his body. You could say that he really loved his body! He had the body building picture of Arnold Schwarzenegger on his wall as he idolized him.

The next thing you know, the gym owner convinced Blake to become an instructor. Why not? Blake was so into body building and cared so much about his own body that he could "walk the walk and talk the talk." He studied their tapes and persuaded me to pay for all his classes. He had me join the gym and life was good. I can remember him telling me one morning that he loved helping people change their lives for the better. The job to him was rewarding. He would say every morning, "I am off to make a difference in someone else's life." It was such a wonderful feeling as a parent to see your child doing something that they love, being happy and most of all, getting PAID for doing something that he loved!

Blake then wanted to expand his instructor skills to actually teaching a workout class. Now anyone that knew Blake, if he had to read anything in Church or get up and give a speech, he mumbled. He was a boy born in Mississippi but grew up down the bayou and he had a flat Cajun accent. "Asking him to teach a class was a bit far-fetched." I thought. "But, he was really into this and his boss must have a lot of faith in him to do the job." That afternoon, Blake was so worked up about teaching the class. He had practiced and practiced. He had all the moves and he felt pretty good. He was ready and then he made his first mistake. He decided to get an energy boost smoothie before class. He was so nervous he had not eaten lunch so he figured he better put something in his stomach.

As the class assembled, he started to get all his gear together including his microphone head piece so that the class could hear him. He had everyone setup to get the class started on time. He was moving good, he thought until... he got to the peak of the workout. He felt his stomach turn. He started sweating and realized, "I am about to upchuck this smoothie!" He dropped his weights and went running for the bathroom. Then he made his second mistake. He left his head gear on. Everyone in the class could hear him losing his guts in the bathroom. He had forgotten about his microphone.

I can remember someone telling me at his memorial service that they were in his workout class and how much they loved him. I just smiled as it comforted me that at the worse moment of my life when my world was turned upside down, someone shared a story. A funny story. I realized God was listening and he made sure to give me something to smile about.

Blake and his beautiful smile

Blake really tried to make a difference in other people's lives as it was so important to him. He wanted them to have hope and reassurance that life is full of hope no matter how horrible the situation maybe. How that one person telling me about being in his class made such a difference to me that day. She gave me comfort as I looked around the Church and I saw all those people he had touched. How he made such a difference in each and every one of them in that room. How at that one moment, when all hope is gone, that one person gave me comfort so that I had strength to make it through that day.

*"Blessed indeed," says the Spirit,
"that they may rest from their
labors, for their deeds follow them!"
Revelation 14:13*

Chapter 31

Flying Fish

By Jesse (Joose) Lagarde

One night we all went tuna fishing in Johnny's boat when BT and I ended up wearing out the crew and the fish. It was around 1 am when me and BT were on watch while everyone was sleeping the flying fish started flying. Tuna was in hot pursuit of these flying fish and we ended up catching some that flew into the boat as well as fighting them. We tried to wake up the crew on the boat, but that was not happening. Me and BT fished all night stepping over people as we caught 100 yellow fin. By the time the crew woke up. We had every fish box full and it was time to go back in as we had caught our limit. It seems like every fishing trip we went on together we had great success, just goes to show you BT was one with the ocean.

Joose, Primetime, Blake (in the background from left to right – Lance Parker and Heath Matherne

"Teach a man to fish, and he will want to buy a boat." Cindie Roussel

Chapter 32

FUMOB

By Cindie Roussel

When I met Scott, I was not really looking to date anyone at the time as I had a mission to get me and my rug rats back to Mississippi. I was tired of being alone and I wanted to get back to my hometown. Scott asked me, "What did Mississippi have that Louisiana didn't?" I replied, "Beaches!"
So one day, Scott decided to take me to Fourchon. We all loaded up in his single cab Ford Pickup truck with our fishing poles.

Blake's First Trip to Grand Isle

The kids were excited as this was an adventure and they did not have to hear Mom tell them we can't afford to do something.
As we drove down Hwy 1, I can remember that salty air smell. That smell is like no other as you know you are close to the water and you

get a since of calmness and peace. It seemed like we had been driving forever when Scott finally said, "We're here." That's when he turned and drove his truck right up on the beach. The waves were crashing over the front of the truck and I began to holler, "Get me out of here! This is no beach! This is the Gulf!" I had never been where you could just drive your vehicle right up on the water. All I could vision was us being pulled out to sea in this F150 single cab truck. I could see the headlines – *"Mother of three children washed away at sea, local trying to show her the beaches of Louisiana."* Well we survived that night and I married him anyways. Anyone crazy enough to drive into the Gulf in his truck to impress a woman and her three rug rats can't be all that bad.

2011 Easter weekend, Blake asked me and Scott to join him and Rachel for the weekend in Fourchon. Now it was sad to say, I had not been to Fourchon since Scott drove me up on that beach. I thought this would be something fun so we said yes. We drove down that morning and met Blake and Rachel at Nobile's camp. We loaded up on the Skank and took off. Blake took us all around the island and then we pulled up at Chris Moran's Marina.

Blake and Scott in Fourchon

I can remember that he jumped out and a young man grabbed the boat and said, "Hello, Captain BT. You need to fill up?" Blake nodded to him yes and the young man jumped on the boat and started filling the tanks. I had no clue the relationships Blake had built down in Fourchon until that weekend. Later that day he took us to Ray and Mary Baudion's camp. I can remember that I was not ready to go home. The day was beautiful and he was so proud to have us there. I can remember him telling us that this was God's paradise for fishing. He said, "Why would anyone want to go anywhere else?" He said, "This is my home and we all take care of each other down here."

Le Paradis De Les pirates
A Pirate's Paradise
Cheryl Terry Cox
(Blake's Godmother, Cheryl painted this picture of Blake leaving Port Fourchon)

I thought back to that day when Scott brought me to the same place and he said the same thing. I never realize until that moment what Scott had given to our children. He introduced them to the world that I may have never given them the chance to see. Had I not let him into our lives, things might have been different. But because God had a bigger plan, Blake was able to see something I could not. He saw the beauty of God's work and he made so many friends in another world that meant so much to him. He referred to the boys from Fourchon, the "Fourchon Mafia", which included Tyler Cheramie, Korte Cheramie, Tony Guilbeau, Dustin Dufrene, Chris Moran, Heath Matherne, Adam Cheramie, Craig Vizier and so many others. They weren't really the Mafia because they were bad ass, even though they might have thought they were, but because they looked out for each other. They were an addition to Blake's Band of Brothers and their world was on the water. "You get in trouble; you could call the FUMOB to come get you," Blake would say.

Heath Matherne (Big Daddy), Blake and Chris Moran

FUMOB

The night Blake went down was the first time I really got to learn who this group was. These are young men who are made of steel but have hearts of gold. They offered up everything they could to help find Blake. Craig offered his house boat to house the search and rescue. Chris offered up whatever anyone needed as far a gas and housing. Heath (Big Daddy) rounded up the boats for the rescue. Johnny offered up his camp and boat.

Like Blake said, these guys took care of each other and I never in my dreams thought I would have to call upon them for help. I love them all and I will always have a special place in my heart for the FUMOB.

**Blake and his racing boat #3
(FUMOB written on the hull)**

Chapter 33

The Mouth Piece

By Tyler Cheramie (T.C.)

It was back in 2002, I was attending my first homecoming party. This party consisted of hundreds of high school kids getting rowdy. Commotion started as Central Lafourche students joined the party. I seen the biggest person at South Lafourche target this long haired fella. As soon as I could blink my eyes, the long haired guy retaliates (after he was pushed) with a smack in the face. Then the fight knocks out all music and the party was over. I wondered and questioned "who was that guy?" Especially to stand up to the biggest guy in the bayou region at that time.

Months passed and the summertime was upon us. Fourchon here we come! We use to congregate each weekend at Tyler Rebstock's camp, near the pool, in Port Fourchon. We were drinking and having a good time, when this long haired fella walked up introducing himself.... "Hey everyone, my name is Blake Terry, they call me BT." as soon as he finished I jumped up saying, "You're that guy from the homecoming party!" "Yep that was me!" Blake replied. We laughed and went through the story and we became to know this long haired fella. When he left, we were all like, that's a cool guy.

The next day arrives all we wanted and did was wakeboard/wake surf! We leave Tyler's camp, idling down the slip, and we see BT at Johnny's camp. We stopped and asked him if he would like to join us. He said sure hold on! He comes running back with his own board (sweet board and bindings) AND a mouth piece? As we headed out we talked as if we had known each other for years. We asked about his mouth piece and he said for his teeth. But we all knew it was a little more than that. We joked saying" you should have grown up down the bayou BT!" Tyler was driving and asked who wants to roll out first? Two second pause, then BT said "if y'all don't mind I'll go." BT gets up on the back and starts strapping in. I will never forget this for the rest of my life. Tyler asked, "BT, hey, you going to wear this life jacket?" BT responds, "No, you can wear it!" and he jumps in with rope in hand and his mouth piece. Once we started pulling him, it was completely obvious why he wore a mouth piece.

Blake Wakeboarding

He was better than any one of us by far. From that day on, we seen each other often and reunited when I had graduated high school and throughout college. It was an honor to call him my friend. I miss and think about him every day. All my love, Tyler (T.C.) Cheramie

Blake and T.C.

"Love one another with brotherly affection. Outdo one another in showing honor." Romans 12:10

Chapter 34

Cowboys like Us

By Russ (Weazal) Guidry and Korte Cheramie

Weazal's story - It was Thanksgiving night 2009 when I received a phone call from Tony Guilbeau saying "Hey, we going to Texas!! Ima pick you up in Baton Rouge in about an hour." I replied "What in Texas? I'm tired!!" He said "Going to Dufrene's ranch... BT's there!!" My response... "I'll be waiting outside my apartment!!"

The Guilbeau brothers and I had traveled the whole night across the entire great state of Texas to pick up, what I can only refer to as 8 ornery horses before meeting up with our padnas in Crockett. There were a few things we knew we had to accept before the trip began — one, sleep was not an option; two, we were gonna have to hunt to survive... either duck, deer or women; three, BT was in Crockett... so we better get our party hats on!!!

We finally met up with BT, Korte, TC, Bread (Guilbeau's cousin) and Dufrene at Dufrene's ranch in Crockett, TX. We saddled up with an abundance of alcohol and smiles ready to go check out Dufrene's newly acquired 6,000 acre ranch. We saddled up and were ready to roll out when Bread's horse went crazy and flung him at full speed against the horse trailer. Once we realized he was ok, we were rolling on the ground laughing. I mean to see the look on his face when that horse took off was priceless. However, BT and I might have laughed a little too soon.

It wasn't five minutes later that BT's horse went crazy and BT went flying. Fortunately for BT his fall wasn't near as bad as Bread's and he got back on and quickly learned how take a firm control over his horse for the remainder of the trip.

Trying to be Cowboys

My horse however, wasn't going to cooperate!! After throwing me off a few times, I decided to give it all I had and take the BT approach and try to make that horse learn who was boss. The horse had other plans... He took off in a dead sprint and I was holding on to the saddle for dear life. The horse ran for about two miles and was not slowing down even though there was a fence about 10 yards ahead of us. I never was so scared in my life!! The horse sharply turned right before the fence and I was able to jump off without a scratch!! It was hilarious and was a perfect beginning to our weekend as "Cowboys."

Korte's story - After a long day of playing cowboy, we decided it was time to make the journey to a local bar to have some fun! Not everybody in the crew was feeling the enthusiasm associated with making the journey, but me, BT, Weazal and Dufrene were ready to give it a try.

184

Weazal convinced TC to let us take his souped up, big dawg, white Chevy HD as long as he drove it there and back.

We were all suited up in our cowboy gear. Cowboy boots, hats, shirts... You name it we had it.

Blake's Boots

BT had bought a pair of new leather boots on the way down just to be ready to impress the ladies. I think Weazal still had his spurs on from earlier that day.

When we rolled up to the bar the locals sniffed us out from a mile away. It was like the music stopped when we walked in and everybody in the bar was asking "Who are those clowns?" Even the bartenders were giving us strange looks when we ordered a round of light beers. It was pretty awkward!! So awkward that Dufrene bailed out on us and he went back to the truck to go to sleep.

The bar was loaded with beautiful women. So, there we were me, BT and Weaz with all these beautiful women and nothing to stop us from having fun. Well almost nothing... The problem was for every beautiful girl in that bar there were at least two hard mean looking real cowboys staring us down like, "I dare one of y'all to try and hit on our girls!!" We regrouped and made a plan to keep an eye out in case anything went down and to have each other's back no matter what... BT said "If any of these guys want to start a fight we were going in FUMOB style... Ain't nobody gonna mess with us!!!"

However, as I mentioned earlier, everyone in the bar knew we weren't real cowboys and they take that stuff pretty serious in Texas when outsiders come in like posers. So, our conventional methods of spitting game wasn't getting us any closer to having fun. We made several attempts to talk to a few girls with no success. Time for plan B... buy shots!! We convinced a few ladies to take some shots with us and as quickly as they took the shots BAM! They were already gone - Straight using us for a free drink! We made our rounds buying shots with several groups of girls and the same thing happened every time!

We were getting nowhere when all of a sudden the prettiest girl in the bar comes our way and BT was all over that. Weaz and I just chilled watching BT work his magic. Her boyfriend and his crew walks up to BT and the girl, grabs the girl and kisses her while giving BT this mean look like he wanted to fight. I looked at Weaz and gave him the nod like we about to throw down with these cowboys... Good thing Weaz had his spurs on cause we were out-numbered 8 to 3!! We approached the group and it was evident that no one wanted any trouble. The night was young and we weren't ready to get arrested just yet, so we left and went back to our corner of the bar.

Feeling defeated by this time, Weaz and I decided it was time to take it to give up and hangout with anyone who was interested. BT, however had plans of his own. Now at this point of the night we pretty much exhausted all of our options. The bar was packed with people, but they were just standing around in their own little groups and nobody really seemed to be having a good time when all of a sudden I noticed everybody's attention was focused on the dance floor. Me and Weaz looked at each other and at the same time said "BT"!!!

The song was "Gettin' You Home" by Chris Young and there he was, BT half-stepping around the entire parameter of the dance floor by himself trying to get the party started. He went across the floor, doing this goofy dance with them cowboy boots that he just bought, like he owned the place. The crowd started to split as he went back-n-forth by himself over the entire floor about four times. When the song stopped, the crowd went ballistic. It WORKED!! Every girl in that bar made their way to the dance floor and wanted a piece of ole BT. Even me and Weaz got on the dance floor and the girls started following us as well since they knew we were with BT. It was crazy!! Every time we looked over at BT he had a different girl he was dancing with... Hell some were even cutting in mid-dance!!

Finally, the night was turning into the party we hoped it would be. We were half-stepping, full-stepping, two-stepping, you name it-stepping all over that bar.

Well the night finally came to an end. The bar was closing and we said our goodbyes. Now all we had to figure out was how to get back to Crockett... Only took us 5 hours for a 45 minute trip!! But no question about it... It was definitely worth it!!

Tyler (T.C.) Cheramie, Blake and Korte Cheramie

Chapter 35

The Godfather

By Cindie Roussel

Blake loved the old characters like John Wayne, Elvis Presley, and Matt Dillon. He had pictures of them all over his house. He also loved the movie, "The Godfather" played by Marlon Brando and Al Pacino, so it was no wonder how excited he was when Dustin asked him to be his daughter, Adrienne's Godfather. Adrienne is Dustin's oldest child. She had a head full of curls with these big beautiful blue eyes with the longest eye lashes that just melted your heart. She had Blake's heart! When she was born, I can remember how Blake put his arms around Dustin as this was the greatest achievement in Dustin's life. Blake was so proud of Dustin and he was honored to be Adrienne's Godfather or as we say in South Louisiana, Paran.

Blake, Dustin and Adrienne

He took the job seriously. He was there to protect her and provide for her. If Dustin needed anything, Blake was there. He loved her with all his heart. She would never need anything as long as she had her Paran; "Pan Pan" is what she called him. Adrienne's first Christmas, Pan Pan bought her a doll that cried and wet. Of course, he threw away the instructions and spent the entire morning trying to figure out how to make this doll cry. He came home with all these toys including this huge play house tent that he played games with. He would tell Adrienne, "Little pig, little pig, let me in." She would holler back, "Not by the hair of my chinney chinney chinney." He would say, "Then I will huff and puff and BLOOOOOWWWW your house in!" She would scream as loud as she could as he would lean over her tent and shake it as hard as he could. She would run out of the tent and say, "Pan Pan, do it again!"

Adrienne and Pan Pan

One time Blake decided to show up at Grandpa Art and Granny Vivian's house as Santa Claus for everyone. When he arrived, Adrienne knew it was him. She could see his eyes and she just knew it was Pan Pan. She was not afraid as little kids are when they see a big man in a red suit and funny beard.

When Dustin and Katy, his wife had their second child, Austin, Dustin had planned for Blake to be Austin's Paran. Never did he dream that Blake would not be here to be a part of his children's life. You just never expect to lose a sibling when you envision your children growing up together.

Austin and Blake

Blake loved children so much and they adored him. He would stop whatever he was doing to find time to sit on the floor and roll around until they both could not go anymore.

I can remember Grandpa Chester loved to eat ice cream and he always had a bucket of ice cream for the kids. He would give each the biggest spoon he could find and they all sat on the floor eating out of that bucket of ice cream. Blake reminded me so much of Grandpa Chester as he would sit and do the same thing with Adrienne.

When Blake died, I put together a shrine, I call it. I have pictures of him on a wall in my dining room and a candle that we light every night. I usually say a prayer when I light his candle. One day Adrienne asked if she could light it and say a prayer. I told her she could as I was not sure what to expect from her. This is what she said,

"Pan Pan, I miss you so much" and then she paused. Then she he put her hand over her heart and said, "I pledge allegiance to the Flag of the United States of America and to the Republic for which it stands, one nation under God, indivisible, with liberty and justice for all."

She looked up at me and asked, "Mimi, do you think Pan Pan liked my prayer?" I replied, "Adrienne, I know Pan Pan LOVED your prayer."

Blake's Shrine

"I call upon thee, for thou wilt answer me, O God; incline thy ear to me, hear my words." Psalms 17:6

Chapter 36

What's In Your Attic?

By Cindie Roussel

When Scott and I met, I really did not know much about the town of Lockport except that the town was small and very family oriented. Everyone knew everyone and I felt safe there. Scott was great about making sure we spent our days doing family fun things together, let's face it, where-ever I would go, I had three rug rats following me. We were a package deal!

Lockport put on two major events, the Holy Savior Spring Fair and the one and only "Lockport Parade." I loved bringing my kids to the fair, but the parade was something like no other. Scott first introduced me to walking the parade, which I thought, "this is crazy? Why would you want to walk an entire parade route when you could be sitting enjoying the parade?" Boy, how I was wrong! In Scott's eyes, why would you want to be a spectator when you could be the star!!!!

I walked my first parade wearing a Merlin costume that made me look about three feet tall. Now, of course I am 4'11" so 3 feet tall did not make much of a difference. That year, I was hooked. I can remember the kids chasing me down the street to hug me. They thought I was this little bitty old man, their height of course. They loved it and I could not get enough hugs. So the next year, I decided to start a theme. We went as the Cone-heads. Then the following year we decided to make real costumes and we went as beer bottles. We started making the costume work for us verses wearing something that would not last. I wanted something for the kids as I remembered how it felt to see them excited about the Merlin costume so the next year, we went as the Simpsons. The kids went crazy over us. Everyone was dressed except for Blake. He was still on the side lines with his friends. We started getting more and more creative and we built ourselves up to more challenging roles – we went as the characters from the Looney Tunes and then Charlie Brown. The children of Lockport thought that Disney was coming to them. I can remember crying when I would turn a corner and hear the children running and yelling, "Stop Lucy, STOP!"

Family fun

Of course it wasn't a kid at all, but a mother trying to save her three year old son as he had grabbed my fake hand hanging from the side to join the group of us and I had no clue he was there. It was a wonder she did not punch Lucy right in the face, but she refrained herself as she was just relieved that her son was not harmed.

My favorite costumes of all were the characters from "Winnie the Pooh!" I could not count how many times I hugged a child as I was Winnie the Pooh that year. It was awesome. I will never forget the feeling of being Pooh and how Disney had really came to Lockport that year.

I really can't describe how wonderful it is to wear a costume like these, but when you put on each and every costume, you feel that you become that character. It is if as though you breathe breath into each one the minute you pull it over your head. I would get tickled every time someone would try on a costume as immediately they would go into this dance. I don't know why, I just know that they would. Something about the character or the feel of being someone else, I am not sure.

Blake soon decided he wanted to join in the fun, but not for Mardi Gras but for Halloween. Halloween was approaching and he decided to dress up but not just in any ole costumes, he wanted to wear original costumes. "Mah, what's in your attic?" he asked. "Blake, I have all my costumes upstairs. You will need to look at them to see what you would want to wear." Of course, I could not throw any of my costumes away as each were characters that were so special to me that I just never had the heart to get rid of them. That was the beginning of "What's in your attic?" call I would get every year around Halloween. Boudreaux, Ponce, Jr. and Joose would show up to look at the costumes. Of all the costumes, they decided to wear one year was the Winnie the Pooh set and they actually won a costume contest. Here's a glimpse into their lives together at Halloween:

Blake and I have dressed up every year for Halloween and ran the streets together. First few years we pulled whatever we could out of Ms. Cindie's attic. Consisting of beer bottles, Charlie brown and friends, the Simpson pez dispensers... And at the age of 23 we did Poo Bear and friends, probably the funniest. We won first prize at a local bar that year. We had a $50 bar tab. I spent it on a bottle of vodka and a huge jar of cherries, instant cherry bombs. I carried this jar, pretzels, and napkins in my honey jar sac. The following year is when we did Ninja turtles for the first time which was a huge hit in Thibodaux. It was great. Jr.

Ponce, Jr., Joose and Blake

Costume making was one of our most favorite times to spend together as a family. As the kids got older, The Lockport Parade became their fun by partying in front of Lockport Junior High and the costume making shifted to Mardi Gras Costumes during Mardi Gras and Halloween costumes for Halloween. I needed to open a factory by now and I was running out of space in my attic. Each time, Blake would ask me right up to the very last minute, "Mah, can you make us some costumes?" I never said no.

Then one year, Blake hit me with this idea he had about a costume I really hesitated to make. He came home with a douche box from the local store. I looked at him like he was crazy. I asked, "Do you even know what that is used for?" "I do now!" he said. He told me that he was buying beer and his buddies dropped about 20 boxes in his buggy. He had no clue what it was for. Then he got this great idea to be a "Douche Bag" for Halloween. Okay, I thought, here I am going from making characters for the children of the Lockport parade to Douche Bag and Tampons. What is the world coming to? Can you see Wally from "Leave It to Beaver" asking his mom, June Cleaver to make him a Douche Bag costume for Halloween? "UH...UH, Mah, I would like to go to this party and uh..uh I need a costume. Do you think you can..uh...uh... make one for me?" "Why of course, Wally. I would love to make you a costume." Oh, and do you think you could make one for Eddie too?

Against my better judgment, I made both Jr. and Blake the costumes. Here is Jr.'s version of the story:

The next year (age 25) is the first time I was worried that I wouldn't have Blake with me for Halloween because he was dating someone and I figured he would do something with her. But he pulled through and we pulled off the best costumes ever. Douche bag and Tampon box took over Frenchman St! No exaggeration when I tell you we took over 200 pictures that night with random people. I remember Ms. Cindie pulled these costumes together that very same day. I don't remember what we did the night before, but I just remember us waking up at my house completely hung-over and me waking up to Blake asking, "Jr., you want blood on your tampon or not?"

Jr. and Blake

The two of them headed to New Orleans in their costumes so proud and so was I. The very next day, I asked, "Blake did ya'll have a good time and how did the costumes turned out?" He said, "Mah, they were a hit! The guys did not understand our costumes, but the LADIES, well they LOVED IT!!"

The following year after Blake died I donated all of my costumes to the local high school. I haven't had the heart to make them anymore, but who knows. Maybe one day I will get that call, that memory from the past but the voice of the future, "Hey, Mimi, What's in your attic?"

More Family Fun

"No pain, no palm; no thorns, no throne; no gall, no glory; no cross, no crown." William Penn

Chapter 37

A Pirate's Life

By Blake Terry

As the seven o' clock alarm goes off and I fall out of my bunk because the six foot side sea is making the boat rock out of control, I ask myself, " What am I doing out here and why do I keep coming back?" My buddy Jared is already cooking breakfast because the sounds of the rig would not allow him to sleep. I walk out on deck to see what the day will be planning ahead of me. As I'm brushing my teeth, Jared ask, "Does that water look like the Mississippi river or is that just my eyes?" I reply, "Looks pretty dirty to me for being as far off the coast as we are." We both sit down and try to enjoy our eggs and toast as the last of our milk spills on the deck. The day is already starting off to be terrible. I look over at Jared to see the same face and say sarcastically, "I can't wait to work in the water we are going to be swimming in today!" He looks back and replies, "I guess that puts us in the same boat huh?" We both laugh at what is ahead of us as we begin to dress in to our wetsuits. We start getting our gear ready and prepare for a long day of diving.

We plunge off the fifty foot mother ship and swim to the "money maker" to begin the fun part of the day. This is a 19 foot rhib boat we use to jump from rig to rig. Jared starts the engine and says, "I sure love the smell of this motor early in the morning." I laugh and reply, "This is what it is all about." We pull up to our first rig and we both jump in to see what the water will do. The surface current is raging almost faster than we can swim. The visibility is extremely cloudy for the first 20 feet. Once we made it past it, the blue water was sitting still like a giant swimming pool with a dark cloud on top. We each pulled 3 mangroves and boarded the "money maker" for our next destination to destroy. "How about that beautiful water with the pea green cloud on top?" I asked. "It's pretty sketchy, but the fish are everywhere", he replies. "We will just have to watch out for each other when we are in the surface cloud", I said with a concerned tone. As our journey proceeded through the morning, we made two loads back to the boat after jumping about 15 rigs.

Blake

It is now lunch time and we are getting ready to fill our bellies for an afternoon hunt. Once again Jared is the master chef fabricating a few ham sandwiches and slices of watermelon for our lunch. "We haven't had any trouble with sharks today for as much blood as we have been stirring in the water", Jared says. "I guess we aren't looking hard enough because we know they are around", I reply as we inhale our lunch.

We finish eating and load our gear back in to the boat to begin our voyage on the afternoon hunt. Once again we plunge back in to the same murky waters, but this time the hunt is not as safe as the morning was. The water has become cloudier and our window of blue water is coming to an end. We managed to keep going with only a 10 foot visibility and a green haze surrounding in all directions.

After two more loads back to the mother ship and a few close encounters with the king of the gulf, Jared looks at me and says, "I think it is time to call it a day. We don't need our greed to take a few limbs with it." I laughed as we plotted our course back to the mother ship. It is getting close to sunset and we have finished washing our gear and hanging it to dry. The waters have calmed down from the morning rollers to almost see your reflection off the back of the boat. I have never felt better after washing off a day of salt water with a fresh shower. The coals on the pit are almost ready for a little surf and turf and the beer has never tasted better. Jared and I both sit back in our hammocks and enjoy the life at sea. I ask, "Sometimes I wonder why we do this to ourselves on a weekly basis?" Jared replies, "Every morning we get up and ask each other the same thing and at the end of the day, we both agree that this is what life is about. A hard day's work with a great day's pay and we are doing what we love the most."

Blake "Catch of the day!"

Chapter 38

Outer Space Underwater

By Blake Terry

Ever since the first time my dad took me offshore fishing, I have always wanted to know what it was like underneath the surface of the deep ocean. It seemed that every time we went fishing, we loaded the boat down with many different species of fish. It made me wonder about life is actually of the ocean. The older I became and the more I learned about fishing, I began to realize that these different species of fish all have their own characteristics and behavior. Then I started focusing on fishing in deeper waters to find bigger fish. I started catching large amberjacks and groupers and my brain began wanting to explore the deep ocean even more. I kept on fishing from my boat with the dream of one day being able to swim with these giant fish myself.

My ambition to become a diver became to strong by the time I turned the age of 16. I went to my local dive shop and purchased my first set of snorkeling gear. I was now finally about to take the first step in pursuing my dream of making my first deep dive. After getting comfortable with my snorkeling gear, I scheduled my classes to get certified in scuba diving. As my diving classes went on, I began to understand that diving to a very deep depth would take some serious training and skill. I was taught that the recreational sport diver should not go past one hundred feet. This started to make my dreams unrealistic at first, but I was not going to give up without putting up a struggle. I finished my in-class training and headed to the Gulf of Mexico to finally make my first underwater exploration.

It was everything I hoped for it to be and more. The fish, along with the coral reef along the structure of the rig, fascinated me.

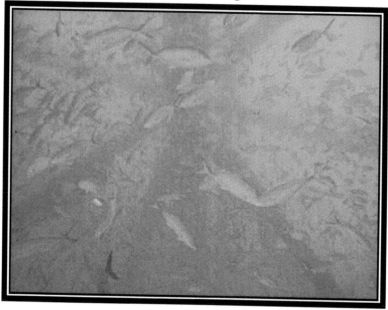

View of Rig

My interest in these underwater ecosystems grew stronger and I began diving every chance I could. Some of my veteran diving partners started coaching me along way. I became more experienced as time went on and I started diving to deeper depths. Then it was like dejavu from my early days of fishing because as I approached deeper depths, the fish grew larger.

I was only capable of going to a certain limit on my depth because I was breathing compressed air rather than a mixture of gases. The deeper I would go, the more nitrogen my body would absorb. I could only go so deep before my air became poisonous to my body. My deepest point was two hundred and twenty feet beneath the surface. The best way I could describe it was it felt like outer space.

The fish around me were of great size, but I was looking down another one hundred feet and those fish were even larger. I knew if I wanted to truly see what was down there; I would have to extend my training more.

Blake Tuna Fishing

My research continued and I found an article online about deep sea diving that interested me. It gave me a better view about the risks involved with deep diving. Technical dives, or deep dives, can range from one hundred and thirty feet to over five hundred feet in depth. Special equipment such as gas mixtures, decompression rules, extensive training, and a level mind are required to perform a technical dive. Most people do not dive to these depths for no reason. They are either exploring something such as a ship wreck or they have to complete a job. Over the past few years, there have been controversies about what type of air to breath in order to reach these deep depths without it becoming poisonous. Some people believe breathing compressed air works as long as the person has a tolerance for nitrogen narcosis. Research has proven that breathing mix gas is the safest way to dive because it prevents the effects of nitrogen narcosis. Nitrogen narcosis occurs when your body absorbs too much nitrogen from diving too deep. One breath at two hundred feet is equivalent to twenty breaths on the surface. Mix gases called trimix are mainly used today for dives deeper than one hundred feet.

As my diving went on, all my questions for the recreational diver had been eventually answered. The next person who came to my mind is a commercial diver. A commercial diver is generally associated with the oil field and spends most of his or her time working under water. Commercial divers are a rare breed of people because their jobs are more dangerous than the average person. I figured the best place for further information about the deep ocean would be from someone who is in that environment every day. The elite group of commercial divers is known as SAT divers. They perform the deep water jobs in the commercial industry. Sometimes they have to stay in the decompression chamber for as long as forty days to clean their bodies because they have to dive so deep. They have seen grouper larger than words can describe. I still find it hard to comprehend even after I have heard them first hand.

My diving partners and I always have talked about what we would see down below our deepest depths. Then one day we read a story about a man that fulfilled the same lifelong dream we all have had. The forty year old man explored a ship wreck that was four hundred and twenty-five feet deep. His reason behind it was to shoot a giant grouper. This was a technical dive that required a team of individuals working together to make his dream happen. It was a dive that was very risky because if one thing went wrong, his life was over. If anything went wrong while he was down there, it had to be fixed right away without panicking since he was not capable of rushing to the surface. The man and his dive buddy had to breathe a mixture of gases so their body would not be poisoned with the wrong gas. They dove down to the wreck and there were grouper everywhere between fifty and one hundred pounds. Then he spotted the giant four hundred and three pound grouper swimming straight towards him. He shot two shafts in his head and killed it instantly. That is something he will remember for the rest of his life.

Although his story sounded too dangerous, he survived and was able to tell the story because of his skills and the support of his crew. Diving down to a depth like that is not the idea of the average person. It takes a level mind along with a great crew to pursue a dream like that. One day I will hopefully be able to fulfill my dream as he did. I have got a few other goals I want to accomplish in life before I take a risk of that nature. Until that day comes where I get to dive on my deep wreck, I will have to keep dreaming of what it would be like.

Blake's Record Tuna – 213lbs
(Photo provided by Toby Armstrong Photography)

Chapter 39

Two Suits A Year

By Cindie Roussel

Blake was always about attending events whether a wedding or a funeral. He felt that it was so important to the wedding couple or to the family of the deceased. That explains the thousands of people that came to his memorial. They all loved Blake as he was so considerate when it came to these types of things. I know some are very uncomfortable about attending funerals, but he always believed it was our responsibility to put the family first. He had faith in a God and he knew our Christian responsibilities in doing what was right in the end.

Every year, Blake would shop for two suits. He would tell me, "Mah, it's time to start shopping." So I would start looking for sales. Of course, Blake would never buy the one on sale; he preferred the best and those usually were found to be the most expensive. He loved a new suit almost like a buying a new toy. He would make sure the suit fit just right, from the shoulders being wide enough to the sleeves fitting perfectly to his wrist. Having these suits ready and pressed just right for wedding and holiday seasons were very important to him. Among the festive seasons was also the thing we don't ever want to prepare for, and that is for funerals. He felt the need to always be prepared no matter what. I really never could figure out this old fashion tradition of buying a suit, except that maybe he got this from his Grandpa Chester who was always prepared. Or maybe it was the fact that he wanted to be prepared to help others and that the suit was just something in his mind that comforted him in being ready.

I can remember that he just bought this pin-striped suit that he was so proud of. He wore it to a wedding and then after the wedding everyone headed to a local bar in Thibodaux. Blake just got to the bar when someone who did not like Blake saw him walk in. Now, Blake may have had a lot of friends, but he seemed to have trouble when it came to fathers of daughters. This person was someone who was a family brother of a father who truly hated Blake. Needless to say, being in the wrong place at the wrong time was what this was and Blake had no clue. About this time, the guy shoved Blake off the bar stool and Blake caught his sleeve on the chair of the stool. He ripped his jacket up the arm of the sleeve. Blake went to hit the guy when the bouncer grabbed him and said, "Blake, you got to get out of here as there's a whole family in here, ready to kill you." So the bouncer eased him out of the bar, but that was not the end of it for Blake. When he got back to the truck, he realized his new jacket was ripped, that was all it took. He headed back into the bar and it became an all up bar room brawl.

The very next day, he asked me if I could fix his new jacket as he was innocently attacked in a bar last night and he had to defend himself. I told him, "Blake, you were in a bar room drinking…I don't see anything innocent about that!" I fixed his jacket.

Rachel and Blake

God tells us in the bible to put on the armor of life. The book of
Ephesians, sixth chapter Verses 14 through 17 tells us, "Stand firm,
with the belt of truth buckled around your waist, with the breastplate
of righteousness in place, and with your feet fitted with the readiness
that comes from the gospel of peace.

In addition to all this, take up the shield of faith, with which you can extinguish all the flaming arrows of the evil one. Take the helmet of salvation and the sword of the spirit, which is the word of God."

Be prepared. Blake was always prepared for the inevitable. Funny as we really never prepare ourselves for a funeral, especially your own child's funeral. I can remember my sister Kathie taking me into a local dress shop to buy a black dress to wear for Blake's funeral. I had lost a lot of weight and I never thought about having to go out and buy something to wear to a funeral. I was not prepared. I can remember falling to my knees in the dressing room thinking I cannot believe I am doing this. "I cannot believe I have to find something to wear to Blake's funeral services? This is so wrong!!!!" as I shouted to Kathie. She just picked me up off the floor and said… "I know…I know."

I know that when Blake felt down at any time of his life, we would talk about what was he doing to make a difference in someone else life? This was our family rule when we needed to get back on track. We lived by the fact that you needed to do for others and then the focus is off of you. As long as you change focus off yourself, you could help someone while God was helping you. Trust in God. Looking back now on this, I can tell you it was very hard to trust God in handling the death of Blake. I had to live by my own rules which were easier said than done. I thought I was a good Christian person until I was put to the test.

Being prepared is so important for all of us. Blake knew that as long as he was prepared, God would handle the rest. Trust in him to do what is needed in helping you. He focused on others and trusted in God. But he also knew that he had to do his part by being prepared no matter what.

216

Chapter 40

The Oil Spill

By Cindie Roussel

"Mah, I feel like a failure." Blake said. "You are not a failure, Blake." I replied. "Just because you are not going back to college this semester does not mean you are a failure." "But Mah, I got to go back. What am I going to do?" he pleaded with me. "You will figure it out, but I am not writing another check for you to party at college." I said firmly.

I can remember that discussion as though it was yesterday. Blake sat in my office the last day of registration at school and I refused to give him a check for tuition. I had written my last appeal letter and I was done paying for him to have a good time and not make the grades. He was so upset with me, but I held firm. So, he stayed out of college his third year and he saved to pay for his next year on his own nickel. It was a tough lesson for him, but he took college more seriously at that point. He finished his third year and headed to UNO in New Orleans until Hurricane Katrina hit. After seeing the devastation, he told me that he was quitting college and heading back to the Gulf Coast to help rebuild. Something in his heart drove him and I was not going to stop him.

The summer of 2008, Blake established his business, Team Terry Marine. He was 24 years of age. He had built his cliental and he had become well known to several business men in the area as they referred to him as "The Boat Doctor." Instead of pulling their boats into shops, he was making house calls. Things were going well and then the worst disaster in our area hit, The Oil Spill!

Blake had already started working on lining up some boats to work offshore and he was doing well for himself. I can remember Scott, Blake and I were headed to a Saints play-off game when Blake was sitting in the front passenger seat talking on the phone with someone while having a beer in between his legs. He was telling the other person on the line, "I need about 4 or 5 boats, how soon you think you can get them to me?" I thought, "Who is this kid?" Then when the oil spill happened, he decided to see what he could do to help. He started making phone calls and the next thing you know, he was signing Master Service Agreements with several local businesses. Johnny Pinell gave him his camp in Fourchon and Blake was hiring everyone he knew. Blake had over 10 vessels running with a crew of about 50 men cleaning oil. He gave anyone he knew a job, they just had to pass a drug test.

That year, Blake's business was strong. He took a disaster that had impacted the entire Gulf Coast region and brought jobs to people who needed jobs. These men slept together, ate together and worked hard together. Blake had setup camps all along Fourchon with boats lined up to support the clean-up effort. He was running these crews during the day and turning wrenches and cleaning engines at night to ensure every boat was running. Scott and I did not see him for several months as his world was the Gulf and we supported him. I would go next door and sit in his house and cry because we missed him so much. But not a day went by without that phone call, "Hey Mah, just checking in. What ch'all doing?" I would tell him, "Missing you, Baby." Then he would tell me how his day was and that he was headed back out into the Gulf tomorrow. "I

Love ya, Mah!" he would say before he hung up the phone. "I love you too, baby!" I replied.

Work Boats for Oil Spill

Team Terry Marine was one of the first responders to helping during the Oil Spill and they were one of the last to come home. Blake never believed in blaming anyone for what happened as this disaster could have destroyed his business. Instead, he took action in claiming what was his and fighting to make things better. After he died, I kept his email and facebook page as I had all his passwords to his things, something he made sure I had. I saw a message on his facebook page one day, "Call me." Then Blake got another message, "I just got out, give me a call!" Then I figured that this person had no idea that Blake was gone. I decided to respond. "Blake died

August 13th, 2011 in a diving accident." This person had no clue. He had just got out of prison. He said that Blake was a close friend and he had no idea he had passed.

Heading out on one of the Work Boats

When Blake gave all those men jobs he did not care about their past or what experience they had. He wanted to give them an opportunity to succeed. Looking back now, I wonder if he remembered how he felt when he could not go back to college. That feeling he felt of being a failure? Did he want to give each and every one of these guys an opportunity to make life better for themselves? You bet he did! Those men loved Blake and most of all, he loved them!

Blake during the oil spill

"Teach me to do thy will, for thou art my God! Let thy good spirit lead me on a level path!" Psalms 143:10

Chapter 41

It's Just an Engine

By Lance Parker

2007 was the first time I went fishing with Blake on a charter fishing trip. We caught nine yellow fins on that trip. I fell in love with fishing after that. I had never went before and Blake was the one to go with. He was the man when it came to fishing! It was amazing to be out there fishing around the rigs. I was fortunate and blessed to have met Blake. Blake and I were a lot alike.

Lance Parker and Blake

We clicked. He took me offshore fishing and I brought Blake in the marsh, speckle trout fishing. When the oil spill hit, I decided to build a boat and he was my main man. I bought a hull from Florida, weld the cabin, and then when it came time to hang the engines, I called Blake. He was running boats and loading boats for both Southern Outdoors and ES&H. He was running all the boats. I would catch him on the fly. He was the type that he had to keep the boats running. If the boat had trouble, he had the mindset that no matter what, that boat is going to run tomorrow. That's why I am so successful today.

My dad and I have been in the business where you are dependent on the mechanic. If they could not get it running, we would have to call our customers to tell them that we can't be there tomorrow, but Blake changed that for me. He would say, "***It's just an engine***, I am going to fix it one way or another. I might have to hot wire something or cut alarm, but that boat is going to be running no matter what." Blake would not give up! That taught me so much. I guess that is why I have excelled in my business. I got several friends that run tug boats and supply boats that if they break down, they are depending on that mechanic. Not me, come Friday and Saturday night I am working, "broke a nut?" I am going back to Thibodaux and then back down to Fourchon to fix it. I got ownership in 5 boats and working seven. That is why I named my last boat after Blake. That is why I am in the business I am in today. My original plan was to stay where I was and run the one boat I bought for the oil spill and then turn it into a party barge. I built it in July and worked it through December 31st. I made enough money to pay off the boat. I always had the entrepreneur in me and then I went after my second boat after talking with Blake. He was my go-to-man and I decided to do it because of him. If I had an engine go down, He would walk me through the steps on the phone. Now I call myself an "oil-change mechanic." I opened another company after that – Southern Marine.

My whole deal came from Blake and watching him. He was so talented with mechanics. We partied together, but mainly worked together. He could pick up on anything. A lot of that is from not being scared. We both were not afraid to tackle anything. I am not afraid to tell everyone that I got my experience from Blake.

Blake and I had laid out a design on how my next boat should be. That is now the Captain Blake Terry named after him. His boat – 42 foot 10 to 12 man cabin with two Yamaha 350 motors, holds 200 gallons water and 200 gallons of diesel. It's like a mini-supply boat. None of the other little boats that I have are built like this one. I think about him daily. We always caught each other on the fly. We would hang out 30 minutes, have a beer, and then head back out to work. Losing Blake was horrible, but I know that there is more to it. Blake loved to help people but now I know he can do so much more. Look at the changes that have happened to so many people that are positive. He was the one guy you met that you would never forget him. He was always the same person, not a fluke. He went down early that I have to think in a positive way; God has a plan for everybody. Blake's not here but he is still working in everybody's lives. Everyone is going to miss him, but this is God's world. Everybody can't have good time like Blake did either. You can try but it will kill you. There is only one person that could live like Blake did and that was BLAKE TERRY. In the end, God will get you through anything. Last time I saw Blake, was at his house. I was passing through to pick up a part. Blake told me Rachel was pregnant. I told him about a men's fraternity bible study that I had taken at Community Bible Church.

Dustin and Blake Jr. (Hank)

We both talked about the right things in life and about God. He told me, "Yeah I am going to get married." He was just as humble as he could be about the whole thing. God had a plan for Blake not to be here though. Blake helped everybody, but he is working way more now than he ever did. He did more good, had more friends; changed more people's lives than a 70 year old man could have ever done in his life time. He lived a hell of a life and I am proud to say he was my friend!

Chapter 42

No Regrets, Well Maybe Just One.

By Cindie Roussel

"Ms. Cindie, is Whitney there?" I heard an unfamiliar voice on the other line. "This is Greg. I work with Daniel." "No, she is at work." I replied. "Is everything okay with Daniel?" "No, we think he had a heart attack." He said with uncertainty in his voice. "Oh my God! Where is he?" I asked. "They are bringing him in the ambulance to Lady of the Sea." "We are on our way." I said and hung up. I called Whitney at a local restaurant where she was working at the time and she started crying. I told her not to drive and that I was on my way to pick her up. It was about 8:00 o'clock in the evening and the roads were dark with very little traffic. When we finally arrived, Daniel was laying on a bed in the emergency room. He was white as a ghost and dizzy.

After several hours waiting, his test came back fine, thank goodness. The doctor told him to meet with a cardiologist to run more test to make sure everything was okay and we were on our way home. I finally dropped of both Whitney and Daniel about 1:00 in the morning and I did all I could to stay awake to get home. I can remember feeling relieved when I crawled into bed about 2:00.

Around 2:30, Scott went flying over the bed to look out the window. "WHATTHA???!" he hollered! "IT'S BLAKE! HE HIT THE TREE IN THE FRONT YARD!" Half out of it, I flew straight out of bed, ran out the front door with no shoes on to see that Blake's truck was wrapped around an oak tree in our front yard. The ground was cold and wet as I ran to his truck. The horn was blowing as the lights were flashing. I am sure about this time, everyone in the neighborhood was up. I pulled the door open and Blake was slumped over in the seat. Both airbags had deployed and ONSTAR was coming over the speaker, "Mr. Terry, are you alright?" I just knew he was dead. "BLAKE", I yelled. The cab was full of smoke from the air bags that at one point I thought the truck was on fire. I pulled him towards me and he said, "Mah, what's wrong?" "Blake, get out of the truck, it's on fire." I yelled.

He climbed out as I pulled him toward the house. He was shook up as he was completely clueless that he had just hit a tree. "Blake, you hit a tree!" I screamed at him. "Mah, I was sleeping, what are you talking about? I don't have a scratch on me?" he replied as he looked down at his body and back at me in disbelief. He then looked back over at his truck and said, "MAH, I HIT A TREE!" In the meantime, Scott is trying to tell ONSTAR that he is okay and that we have it all under control. He tried to convince them not to send an officer out but they had to due to the air bags deploying. Blake then does the unthinkable. "I can't get another DUI, I am running!" He said. "WHAT?" I HOLLERED. "YOU CAN'T RUN. YOU HAVE YOUR TRUCK WRAPPED AROUND THE TREE IN THE FRONT YARD. HOW ARE YOU GOING TO RUN?" I SHOUTED! About that time, the police show up and Blake is gone. We have no idea where he is and we are trying to explain to two police officers that we have no clue where he went. They search his house and then around the property. I decide to call Whitney and Dustin as I needed some help. The tow truck shows up and finally the officers give me there information and tell me that Blake has 24 hours to call in or they will serve him with a warrant. As they are pulling out, Dustin and Whitney arrive. We all go in the house wondering where the hell Blake is. As soon as the officers pull out and the coast is clear, Blake comes through the back door of the sun room. He is covered head to toe in mud. He looked like he was in a war movie where all you could see was the white of his eyes. He had been hiding in the bayou waiting for the helicopters and dogs to show up, but they never came. "Mah, burn my clothes so we can get rid of the evidence." He said. He stripped down naked in front of all of us and then he took a shower in Scott's bathroom. Dustin and Whitney put him in the back of Whitney's car and made him lay down out of sight just in case the law was patrolling the area for a wanted man on the run for hitting a tree in his own front yard. Blake never had many regrets, but I do believe that was probably the one he would have admitted to. He had bought his truck on New Year's Eve and wrapped it around a tree January 28th. He had not paid the first note on his truck yet. When he went to court, the judge looked at him and dismissed the case. He knew that Blake would have to pay to fix his truck and he seemed to have some compassion for him as the only thing that was really hurt in all of this was Blake's check book. On the other hand, the Judge did tell him that the real reason he dropped the case was because Blake wore a tie in the court room that day.

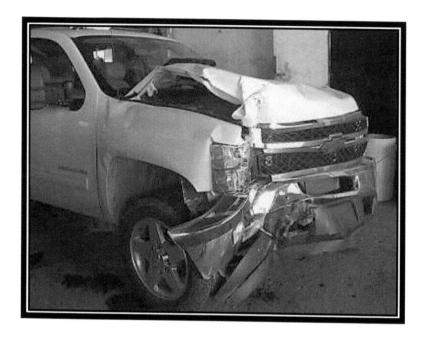

Blake's one regret!

Chapter 43

Hemingway Code Hero

By Blake Terry

We all encounter many different experiences life has to offer on a daily basis. These experiences allow us to make decisions that we either may benefit or suffer from. Some of us handle these experiences better than others. While growing up among our crowd of friends, most of us have had a hero involved inside our group. The person who always seems to handle the situation, no matter what it may be, in a better manner than the rest of the crowd. This person is normally the leader of the bunch. A person who his companions can look up to and follow his or her lead. While at the same time, the leader never puts his or herself above anyone else in the group. Ernest Hemingway shows this type of behavior in some of his characters in the novel, "The Sun Also Rises." He demonstrates different acts of what he considers heroism throughout the novel.

The Hemingway Code Hero has many unique traits that separate him from the ordinary person. A Hemingway Code Hero acts gracefully when under pressure. Facing death is the only way a Hero may face himself. Someone who can respond to an emergency just as quick as the emergency arises is considered a hero. Not only can they respond in time, but they can do it in a graceful manner in order to keep the situation as calm as possible.

For Hemingway, the greatest trait in a man is his own self-discipline. This is someone who can always maintain his or her composure, even when the circumstances become extreme. The Hemingway

231

Code Hero is also a person of some degree of skill. This is a skill that separates that person from the rest of the crowd

I enjoyed Hemingway's novel because he seems like a decent man through his writings. He writes about drinking in bars and beautiful women. I enjoy reading things I can relate to. I would consider myself to be one of his heroes. I tend to keep my composure in tight situations. There is no room for error when diving offshore.

Blake, Flo, Joose, Jr. Rachel, Boudreaux, Tia, Stephanie and Ponce

The first thing that comes to mind in an emergency is to react rather than to panic. I tend to lose composure occasionally when I have had too much to drink but I also believe to have some skill too when I am intoxicated.

Since they both cancel out, I guess I   am still a Hemingway Code Hero.

"Facing death is the only way a Hero may face himself." Blake Terry

Chapter 44

I Love You This Much

By Cindie Roussel

"I love you this much" as Blake would hold out his arms wide and give me a hug. This was something each of my children would do when we would talk about how much each of us loved each other. "I love you more than the trees, the sky and the heavens...I love you this much."

Going through the loss of a child or loved one, you really put that love to test. Scott and I seemed pretty happy, I thought before Blake died. We had our ups and downs like any normal family did but we really thought we were strong as a family and that nothing could tear us apart. Then our world turned upside down. We hurt so much that comforting each other was just too difficult.

Parents who suffer the death of a child are more likely to divorce according to some statistics. In fact, the often-quoted statistic is that 75 percent of parents eventually divorce within months of the loss of a child. However, that number was of a book author who wrote about this back in 1977. Studies conducted since then paint a different picture. The Compassionate Friends, the nation's largest self-help bereavement organization for families who have experienced the death of a child, conducted a survey in 2006 that showed a divorce rate of 16 percent among bereaved parents.

In another study, researchers at Montana State University-Billings administered a survey to parents who had suffered the loss of a child.

The results? Nine percent of the respondents divorced following their child's death. And 24 percent of the remaining respondents had considered divorce but had not actually done so. So in 33 percent of the couples taking the survey, the death of a child had stressed the marriage, but the divorce rate was nowhere near 75 percent. All I know was that we were a close family prior to losing Blake and now we were a statistic. How were we going to survive this if we could not hold onto each other because of our pain?

One night, Dustin made a comment for me to not give the kids so much ice cream and I completely lost it. I went storming out the room in tears and Scott came running after me. He grabbed my arms and said, "Cindie, you have got to stop fighting this and talk to me." I was a basket case. I wanted everyone to leave me alone and I did not think I could love anyone at this point.

Finally one day, I told Tina, that I did not think that Scott and I were going to survive this. My life felt like it was falling apart. She tried to reassure me but I know that she did not have the answers for me. Tina was not just my assistant but a very close friend. Her daughter, Reesa had dated Blake for several years during their college days, so she knew Blake very well. I asked her to have her mother pray for me as Ms. Hazel Cheramie or as some call her, Maw Hazel, was a traiteur. A traiteur is a Cajun healer who practices what is sometimes called faith healing, or else a traditional healer of the French-speaking Houma Tribe, whose primary method of treatment involves using the laying on of hands. She told me, "Of course. Maw Hazel will have the answer, I am sure."

The next day, Tina came into my office and gave me a prayer that Maw Hazel asked her to give me. She then said something that made no sense to me. She said, "Maw Hazel wants you to hold Scott in your arms tonight when you climb into bed." I thought, are you nuts? I don't feel like talking with anyone let alone hold anyone. However, Maw Hazel had been married for over 50 years to Robert (Pa Robert) so she had some experience in holding on to a husband.

As I read the prayers, I did not quite understand the meaning but I read them over and over. She gave me Psalm 139 Verses 1:24 – "*O Lord, you have searched me and known me…you have hedged me behind and before, and laid your hand upon me. Such knowledge is too wonderful for me; it is high, I cannot attain it…Search me, O God and know my heart; Try me, and know my anxieties; and see if there is any wicked way in me and lead me in the way everlasting. And then Isaiah 57:18– I have seen his ways and will heal him. I will also lead him and restore comforts to him and to his mourners. I create the fruit of the lips; peace, peace to him who is far off and to him who is near.*"

That night when Scott and I climbed into bed, I read the prayers again and I turned off the light. I rolled over to his back side and placed my arm under his arm and pulled him close. I heard him start to cry and he rolled over and we both cried together. I am not sure what happened except that God understood our pain and his knowledge is above us to understand. Scott hurt like I did and he could not comfort me and I hurt too much to comfort him. God understood this and he gave the answers through Maw Hazel. Maw Hazel was given a gift to help others and she shared her gift to both Scott and I.

Psalm 139 verse17, "*how precious also are your thoughts to me, O God! How great is the sum of them! If I should count them, they would be more in number than the sand; When I awake, I am still with you.*"

When I could finally hold my husband again I felt so much love that I knew I was finally awake. I was no longer in that dark lost place but I was able to hold onto something that was stronger than I could describe. I felt God's presence for the first time since Blake had died.

"I love you this much" is something I continue to pass on to my Grandchildren as I hope that they know just how powerful love can be. I hope my children know how much I really do love them and most of all I hope my husband knows just how much I love him. Not by the words of saying, "I love you," but at night when I place my arms around him, he knows that when he awakes that I am still with him and most of all, he is still with me.

Me and Scott

Chapter 45

The Last Dive

By Jonathan Nobile

Blake and I had been fishing for three days aboard the Sea Quest when we pulled up to "Lobster" (EB 873). We decided to make a quick bounce dive for grouper before it got dark. We got our gear together and suited up for the dive. We both had 2500psi of air in our tanks - 500psi short, but no big deal since we have done "a lot worse on a lot less." The dive plan was to drop down to 200ft, stick a couple of grouper, come up to 60ft and look for lobster.

We splashed down and began our descent. We were side-by-side the whole way down and everything seemed to be fine. When we hit 200ft, the visibility became very poor due to the lack of light and the nitrogen narcosis was coming on heavy. You could see up, but you couldn't see down. The visibility was about 15-20ft. Blake and I were side-by-side when I spotted 2 groupers. One took off, but I was able to make a shot on a decent sized scamp. He went into the conductors, but I was able to pull him up and out. I was about 10ft above Blake at that time. He was not chasing any fish, nor did I see any more grouper. I kicked up a little while trying to get my grouper under control. When I looked down, Blake was following me up. I got to about 160ft and when I looked down I did not see Blake - only a stream of bubbles coming from where we had just been. This has happened before; I can see his bubbles, he is right there, and he will be up in a second. I never heard a spear gun fire. I waited and waited. I'm not sure how long I waited, but once my mind told me to go see what's going on, I headed back down to see if he was okay.

239

I followed his bubbles back to around 200ft, maybe deeper. My depth gauge only went to 200ft, so I'm not sure how deep I went since I was not wearing a computer. The light was cutting out and it was very dark and the narcosis was heavy in my head. I noticed the bubbles I was following were very small, and I questioned if this was something from the rig because this doesn't seem like bubbles Blake would make. Had he ascended on the other side of the conductors? I swam up to about 140ft and looked up and out, scanning every bit of the rig I could see. No Blake. I went back down to about 180ft to see if I could find the bubbles I had seen earlier, but they were gone and this was about as far as I could go down without the light cutting out completely. I was low on air and I knew my bottom time was up. I headed up, praying to see him looking for lobster at 60ft and wondering what the hell I had been doing down there. I scanned the water the whole way to 25ft and I did not see a sign of Blake. I had to make a short safety stop which was only a minute or two, max. This was the longest minute of my life. I prayed that I would hit the surface and I would see him climbing on the boat.

Once I hit the surface, I began to scream to the boat, "Where's Blake!!?" When the crew on the boat threw up their hands and said they had not seen him, I knew he was gone and something must have happened when we were ascending. I immediately told the crew to grab another tank. I couldn't go back down because of the nitrogen in my body, but Alex grabbed my gear and splashed down to go look for Blake. This was the quickest I have ever seen anyone swap gear and splash back down. Alex could only make it down to about 70ft before the light cut out on him. After about 10 minutes, Alex surfaced with no luck. In the mean time we scanned all around the rig to see if he had been washed out by the current. Mr. Mark called the Coast Guard, gave them our position and notified them that we had lost a diver. They were sending a cutter and a chopper ASAP. It was now dark and shock began to set in. The next thing I can remember was calling Louis and Rafe to see if they could help. The next call was to Ms. Cindie, Blake's mom.

Blake and Nobile

Blake was my best friend and brother, I miss him so much. He would not want us to cry for him, just "tighten up" and keep on Rollin. I am so honored to have had the pleasure of calling him my friend. He was one of the most interesting and genuine people I have ever met. He will forever live in my memories.

Nobile and Blake

Chapter 46

A Pirate's Farewell

By Whitney Terry Fletcher

It was Saturday at 8:43 p.m. and I had two missed calls from my parents' house. My first thought was, "I'm married and they still freak if I don't answer immediately when I travel." I had just sat down to eat a steak dinner my husband cooked for me in thanks for coming to visit him while he was working out of town. When I called back, Mrs. Necole, the next door neighbor answered the phone. She told me very calmly that Blake had gone diving and hadn't come back up. I had to have said something about being on my way because Daniel, my husband, was out the door telling Greg, his boss, that we were leaving. I must have been vague though because when I stepped outside and Greg asked what was up, Daniel looked at me. I said it exactly as Mrs. Necole did. I couldn't fathom thinking about it yet. I knew how deep he dove. I knew there was no room for error, but it just couldn't happen to Blake. It simply couldn't. He wasn't a dumb adrenaline junky. He was always in control. He was the diver who taught other guys how to dive. I was going to get a call back in two minutes saying it was a mistake.

The last comment I remember hearing before closing the car door was Greg telling Daniel, "Don't rush. You getting there any faster won't change anything." Daniel rushed anyway - enough to get us pulled over before I had even started calling people back. Daniel talked his way out of the ticket and put on his flashers and drove away just as fast as before. I don't remember if Mom called me or I called her back, but she was the person I spoke to next. She told me he was diving at 180 feet with Nobile and Nobile shot a fish and when he turned around, Blake wasn't there. She said the Coast Guard had been called but they were in 900 ft of water. Dustin was already at Moms and he and Rachel were about to leave to go to Fourchon but he wanted to talk to me first. He got on the phone and just said "we both know the reality of this shit, but dammit, I'm going to get him." I already knew that he meant he was going to recover his body and not find a healthy breathing Blake, but none of us could say it yet. The only one left to call was Dad. He didn't know yet. I tried calling but he didn't answer, so I called Jessica, my stepsister. She couldn't fathom this either. She just said, "I'll find Tony. I'll make sure he knows." We hung up. Two seconds later I get a call from Dad and apparently someone got in touch with him. All he could say was, "I don't know what to do Whitney. I'm just numb. I just don't know what to do." I can't even remember what I told him. I didn't know what to do either. The whole ride back I simply balled my eyes out while Daniel made the best time back home he ever did. He called his Mom and his friends to ask for prayers. We didn't know what we were praying for yet...maybe that this was all just a bad joke somehow. Maybe he was sitting on a nearby rig. Maybe because it was nighttime, he was floating 100 yards out and they just couldn't see him. You have the denial because it hurts too much to let your heart believe what your brain already knows.

We arrived at Moms in record time and walked into the sunroom. Mom and Scott were sitting at the table just staring ahead while Donny and Necole, their neighbors, sat there trying to think of what else they could do. I don't even think we hugged. We just walked in and sat down staring at the phone waiting to hear anything. Not long after Jacque and Debbie, my parents longtime friends, showed up then Aunt Kathie, Uncle Wilfred, and Candace. With every person, the tears just poured and the reassurances that he was alive somewhere came out. We all knew better, but who's going to say it first? More people just kept coming and coming. Daniel and I just sat on the sofa until dawn, occasionally pretending to sleep when someone told us to. When the sun came up and the Coast Guard didn't see him, we all knew the final hope was gone. Blake had died. My blonde, bull headed, drunkard with a heart of gold of a brother was gone. I wouldn't hear that laugh anymore. God he had a laugh that made you want to laugh with him and a grin you just knew he was up to no good.

Everyone seemed to need something to do next and obviously, we couldn't just sit back and let the Coast Guard do all the searching. The more eyes out there, the better, right? We had friends galore coming out and dive teams getting boats ready to be at the rig at dawn to have our own search party. We learned that the Coast Guard didn't have tank divers and since he was diving, he was wearing weights. There was no chance, unless he ditched his gear, which was unlikely, he would have floated back up like normal people do a few days after they drown. Divers were the only option in being able to find him and luckily, Blake had a lot of diving friends. Our hope was that he got caught up in the rig's support or piping and didn't sink all the way down. It was a big hope at the time. We were sure he was just right there and we'd pull him up within an hour. No one shared their fear with the group that we might not find him at all. We also had friends on the surface helping search along with the Coast Guard. Those of us still on shore were getting broken reports of what the dive team and search parties were doing.

The Coast Guard kept in touch with Mom until she couldn't answer anymore. When she couldn't hear the bad news anymore from the Captain of the boat, I took over the phones. Often, we knew from our own search party what the Coast Guard was doing before they called us. The dive teams dove to 200 feet and did a full search by 10 a.m. and came up with nothing, but the water was clear as it could be and they were going again. The second search went just like the first. No luck. At one point, Mom saw on someone's phone a text message that said the Coast Guard had called off the search. She came hysterically crying into the kitchen saying, "Why can't they find my baby? Why can't they find him?" My Uncle Ty was standing next to me when that happened. Thankfully he grabbed me in a hug because I don't think my knees could hold me anymore. Not long after that, I answered the call from the captain of the CG boat. Looking back, I see how difficult that call must have been for him and I'm glad I'm the one who took it because I let him off easy. He said they were coming in and they could refuel and go out again, but they had already covered more miles than he could have possibly even swam and with Blake's weights on, the likelihood of them finding him was low. I told him I understood and that we appreciated all they did but there was no reason to refuel. We were going out again the next day with a Remote Operating Vehicle (ROV) and would call if there was anything else they could do. Someone donated us an ROV for the day and we were sending it down to the 900 feet bottom to search.

Dustin drove Blake's truck up from Fourchon that night. It was the first time we'd see each other knowing our trio was now down to two. I watched for him at the front door and met him outside. We just sat there and held each other. Our big brother had gone and left us on our own. What on Earth were we going to do without him?

Daniel and I could not sit around Mom's house any longer waiting. We needed to be on the boat in the morning with the ROV. We needed to see where he went down. So, that night we headed out to Craig's camp to meet up with the search party. This is the first time

I saw Dad. Funny how when two people who see each other are hurting so bad, no words can come out. It's just tears and hugs that don't let go. The camp was full of good friends and after the hugs and tears, the stories began to come out. Jr. and his sister were there along with Lucy, Dad's wife, and we all sat around telling whatever funny story came to mind. Ronnie and Tammy, longtime friends of Dad, had quite a few since Blake often stayed there when going to Mississippi. Ronnie taught Blake as much about truck motors as Dad and our uncles did about boat motors. When Ronnie got the call from Dad about Blake going missing, there was no other place he would be besides at Dad's side helping him find his lost boy. The next morning was the first of many where I learned what it was to go to bed so emotionally exhausted that you couldn't come up with a tear if you tried, but the mornings gave you a reboot and you seem to just wake up with your pillow already soaked in tears.

We were supposed to leave with the ROV at dawn, but as usually happens, we were running behind. While waiting at the camp, a newspaper reporter had gotten my number and wanted to talk to me about running a story about Blake and what happened. After getting the family backing, I called her back and told her all I knew. Telling her what happened to Blake was surprisingly easy, but telling her about who he was, talking about him in past tense, well, that was just torture. I realized later that I hadn't even remembered to give her my married name. I told her my name was still Whitney Terry. Daniel still makes fun of me for that.

So finally, around 10 a.m., the ROV and the boats were ready to roll. Off we went on the two hour journey to Rig 873. It was beautiful. Living in south Louisiana, the water is always brown and murky, but out there, it's blue and clear. It doesn't take long to understand why he loved it so much. We pulled up to the rig and while waiting for the ROV to get set up, Dad, Dustin, and me sat on the side of the boat and just talked. We talked about racing without him and how we were going to make sure baby Hank knew just how great his Dad was. None of us volunteered to be on the boat that the ROV feed was going to. While we all wanted to be there when we found him, I don't think any of us could handle the image of finding him underwater. After a while, we realized the ROV was still not in the water and must be having issues.

First, the issue was the generator powering the ROV. The generator that worked perfectly before we headed out now needed to be rigged up to just get through the day. Second, after about 30 minutes of searching, the ROV got caught up in a bunch of fishing line and had to be untangled at the surface. We get that fixed and back down to the bottom the ROV goes. We heard a call went in to the rig from a nearby vessel that they thought they saw a dive tank floating in the water. We got the coordinates and off we went searching. Our hope skyrocketed. Dad, still in his denial, even started rationalizing how Blake could have lived for the last two days. Ronnie took that one for us by saying, "Let's find the tank and we'll go from there." We called the Coast Guard back and told them the coordinates and everything but when we got there, nothing but clear water.

We started doing a small grid search but the longer we went, the more information started to come in on the tank's description. The tank the other boat saw wasn't Blake's tank. Not even close. When we headed back to the rig to find out after searching the bottom, the power cord to the ROV snagged on something and was irreparably damaged. The ROV guy was in awe of the issues he encountered that day with his equipment that he had never dealt with before. Dustin, Daniel, and I thought we knew why. Blake didn't want to be found. He had always said that if he died out there, leave him there. There's no place he'd rather be anyway. We said as much to Dad and with tears in his eyes he agreed. Sunset was just a half hour away and we decided to sit out there and enjoy a sunset at the rig. We all opened up two beers and drank one for ourselves and gave one to Blake.. Dustin and I rode the whole ride back on the bow of the boat. The one thing we both can remember telling each other is that Blake went out on top. He did not have a grudge with a single person. Everyone knew how much he cared about them and Lord knows he died at his happiest. He was going to be a Dad himself, and he was always fishing, as often as his bank account would have allowed.

The next day was Tuesday and Daniel went to get Izzy, our dog. I had boarded her for the weekend to visit him and we just extended it until then. She's a lab with the energy that fits her breed and the amazing thing was she knew how sad I was. She greeted me, then instead of running around for the next 20 minutes, she just layed down next to me and put her head on my lap. Few things comfort you more than the love of your dog. It was sitting there crying with her I realized that a funeral needed to be planned. A little mental calculation and I realized it was going to be me planning it. Mom, Scott, Dad, Dustin, and Rachel just weren't capable. Parents shouldn't have to bury their children. Dustin didn't have the organizational skills on his best day and Rachel was just too new. Not to say that she and Blake didn't love each other, but I know couples who have been married for years and still don't know what their spouse would want in their funeral plans. It's just not something people want to talk about. I remember looking at Daniel and saying "I'm going to have to do this aren't I?" He just gave me a sad smile back and said, "Yes baby, you are."
We headed to Mom's house and I sat in the sunroom with Daniel, Aunt Kathie, and a few other people and I had them help me with what plans needed to be made, as I wasn't really sure what planning

a funeral service entailed. I didn't start making phone calls though until Dad arrived and I could talk over the arrangements with all of the family. This was Tuesday and Dad and Mom hadn't seen each other yet. Dad was busy with the search in Fourchon, and Mom and Scott were holding up at their house which seemed to be Grand Central Station for anyone who knew Blake, or so we thought at the time. We learned later at his funeral that we had no idea just how many people knew and loved Blake. Dad arrived not long after and his only words to Mom were, "I tried to bring him home to you. I tried so hard." Two people who had been divorced for 23 years and while they didn't bicker like divorced couples do today, they definitely weren't what you call friends. They just sat there on the sofa next to each other holding hands for the next few hours while we all began to discuss what to do next. I brought up having a memorial service and Grandma immediately asked what kind of service. Grandma is staunch Catholic and anything less than a full mass service would just be sacreligious to her. Dad piped in "Mom, it'll be wherever Cindie wants it to be," but mom just smiled at Grandma and said, "Of course it would be Catholic." I think we all knew that Blake wouldn't have really cared either way, but he would have been highly disappointed in us if we let Grandma down.

So I called Holy Savior, the church we all grew up in, but no answer. After a few tries, I began to get worried that we wouldn't get the day we wanted, so I called our friend Sarah who is active member in the church. Sarah and her brother Tim lived across the street from our house on Romy Drive. We were like family as we spent many afternoons together after school not to mention the number of holidays we shared. Sarah's Mom, Mrs. Kathie also has a wonderful singing voice, so I mentioned asking her Mom to sing the hymns for us. She said she'd do what she could. Apparently Sarah had gotten on the phone because about ten minutes later, I received a call back from the priest. He said, "I was told that I was to call you right now under any circumstances, including stopping Mass. How may I help you?" I laughed and gave an inwards thanks to Sarah and set up our appointment with the priest and booked Friday for our services.

Next, I called Granny. I wanted give the family a little peace and offer food and refreshments at our local KC home instead of having everyone come back to Mom's house after the services. I didn't know who to call for that, but my Granny had done it after my Pawpaw's funeral, so I knew she'd know where to start. When I called and asked her about it, she simply said, "I'll take care of it." I'd realize later that this was the only time I called one person one time and the entire thing was taken care of. I'll be forever thankful to my Granny for that.

We then decided we should do a ride out to the rig on Saturday and say our goodbyes there. Not everyone was on board to go, but enough people were, so the plan was to have the ride to the rig, followed by a get together at Flo's camp where we could do a goodbye on the water there for those who didn't go to the rig. Dad then had his job of getting boats ready, so off he went to Fourchon to make it happen. Mom, Scott, Rachel, and I were pushing further into making the arrangements happen, but our house was still full of people who just needed to help. Someone thought of the picture boards Blake had hanging in his house and said we should make more of those. We weren't going to have a coffin to put things in because Blake would have killed us to spend money on something he would have said was useless, so all we could have as a place to pay your respects were pictures. Well, the photo albums came out. Facebook pictures were printed and before we knew it, the house had literally thousands of pictures of Blake and people were trying to narrow down which ones to use. In the end, we decided to screw narrowing it down. We'll just buy more cork boards to put more pictures on. The more pictures we had, the more stories came out. Stories ranging from sweet to something your mother would never want to know. We all began to laugh. Pictures capture just a moment of a memory, but those memories become precious. At one point, the guys thought they should go to Blake's house and take out those things you don't want your mother to find. Mom just laughed. Blake never did feel the need to hide anything from anyone. He was the same person no matter who he was with.

On Wednesday, Mom, Scott, Rachel, and I left the house filled with people to go make all of the arrangements. First stop was the funeral home where we wanted to buy their memorial cards. I think we ordered 300 thinking that was plenty. Next we were off to the church. Rachel was a little uneasy walking into a Catholic church as she was just showing at barely over 4 months along and no wedding band. Little did she know that's not what the priest would have a problem with. We sit down with the priest and begin the easy parts. We wanted a three hour wake time, as surely that would be long enough. Begin things at 8 and have the mass for 11. Then we get into the readings. Rachel had already gone through a few she liked and began to say so when the priest gave us a list of options to use. Before Rachel looked at the list, she said, "I just kinda like these readings because I really don't want the services to be those generic readings you hear at every funeral." Apparently, this was the WRONG thing to say to the priest. He went into his spill of no funeral service is "generic" (Yes, he used hand quotes here) as the Catholic church established these guidelines over thousands of years and the way they do things are handed down from the Pope himself. Rachel was just about to move her stage of grief from depression to anger, so Mom, Scott, and I decided it was time to roll out. We told the priest we'd look over the options and let him know and got out of dodge before

Rachel could tell the priest just where to put his guidelines. Luckily, both of her readings were options on the list, Rachel did not have to settle for generic funeral services.

On the way home, I decided to start calling the newspapers to get an obituary printed. The local paper had already run the story of his accident, so all they needed was me to send in the write up. Great. Next, I call the paper in New Orleans, and the lady asked me what funeral services we were using. I told her we weren't using a funeral home as it was actually a memorial service. She said, "Ok well then I'll need a copy of the death certificate before I can send the obituary to print." I then explained that we didn't have one as he had gone missing on a diving expedition and his body wasn't recovered. Her exact words back were "Well I can't print an obituary without that. I mean, he might not be dead." What?? Excuse me? I lost it on her. I said "Well considering he went missing at 180 feet below the surface in 900 foot of water, unless he became a merman, I think we're pretty confident that he's dead" Mom, Scott, and Rachel looked at me like what the heck is going on? The lady then got a little nicer with me and said she had rules she had to follow- yada, yada, yada. I hung up on her after that. The next newspaper gave me the same issue. Are these people kidding me? Not only do I have to make funeral arrangements for a brother I didn't even get to say goodbye to, I'm having to argue with people about whether or not he's actually dead??? I walked into Mom's back yard, grabbed a ball and Izzy and threw that thing for her to chase until I couldn't throw anymore. I was about to have a nervous breakdown arguing with a perfect stranger about my brother being dead when I myself couldn't believe it yet. I couldn't lose it. People still needed me to finish this. So instead of crying, I just threw a ball relying on my tireless dog to keep me together a little longer. When I thought I could handle it, I went back inside and told Daniel what was up. He said, "Well they asked you what funeral home you were using right? So, just call the funeral home you bought the cards from and have them call the newspapers." He was right. Maybe they wouldn't question it if it came from a funeral home instead of me. Called up the funeral home and they were happy to assist. This worked for two of the three newspapers that gave us issues and that was good enough for us. I wrote up his obituary that night and sent it out to all of the newspapers. It's been two years since his death and I still can't even look at an obituary without remembering just how hollow I felt having to write that.

Thursday was full of people putting pictures on cork boards, going to local store to buy up every easel they had, and then finally going shopping for outfits to wear to the funeral. Daniel, Katy, and I went shopping together. We got Daniel his first real suit. Katy and I went to the baby section and found the cutest suit and dress shoes for Austin, who was only 9 months old. I don't remember buying my dress or Katy buying hers. I know I had to try it on at some point, but none of this has stayed in my memory. Maybe it was just too hard. I do remember going back to Mom's that night and everyone having a competition for who can put easels together the fastest. The men can say what they want; the women dominated that project. We had also needed a good large photo of Blake for the front centerpiece. We couldn't seem to find anything of high enough quality to get it blown up, but then I remembered my wedding photos. Daniel and I had just gotten married in March, so they were as recent as you could get. There was one photo that was a group shot with Daniel, Me, Dustin, and Blake, but Blake looked great in it. So I called my photographer and asked him if he could blow that part of it up for me. This was about 3 in the afternoon and he normally closed at 5. He told me to come at 5 and he'd do what he could. I will always recommend Picture Parlor photography because not only did he enlarged that shot, he photo shopped it to remove any spots where the rest of us we were in the picture, and fixed the background because he said it clashed and he wanted it perfect for me. He then handed me a gorgeously done photo and said, "There's no way I could charge you for this." He and his wife remembered Blake from my wedding and they said he seemed like the greatest guy you could know.

The funeral services began Friday morning. Daniel and I seemed to get dressed so slowly. We just couldn't seem to bring ourselves to get in the vehicle and go knowing we were going to have to officially say goodbye. We arrived at the church at quarter til 8. Holy Savior church has an aisle 100 feet long, and we had enough flower arrangements to go down both sides of the aisle along every other pew. Plus some in both of the churches entrances and of course, some up at the altar. This should have been our first sign of what was to come. We had set up the picture boards at the entrance to the church so people who were waiting to pay their respects had something to look at. Thank God because if we would have set those up at the altar with us, the line would have never moved. The people who just kept coming was something none of us will ever forget. By 8:15, the line was out of the church and into the parking lot. By ten, the cops were called because people were parking in driveways of houses nearby since there was no other parking anywhere. Most friends told us they waited about an hour to an hour and a half to see us. Outside, in the hot August sun, in suits and black dresses, these people waited just to say, "I'm so sorry you lost him. We loved him too." We set up the guest book at the front entrance, but the line moved its way out of the side entrance, yet still, we had over 1000 signatures. When the lines ran out, people signed in the margins. And we thought 300 cards would be enough. When the line was still going strong at noon, an hour after we were supposed to have Mass, the priest finally came up and told people to please just sit down so we could try and get started. I hugged more sweaty necks that day than I could in a lifetime and I'm thankful for every one of them. For everyone who stood there and just reminded me that there were so many others who knew just how wonderful he really was.

The services began with Mrs. Kathie and Hannah singing the most heartfelt version of "I Can Only Imagine" by Mercy Me. Rachel had picked the song and I had always thought it to be a bit cheesy. Well coming from those two women, I was wrong. There was not a dry eye in that place. I felt bad that we made the boys do their eulogies right after. Had I thought about it, I would have switched up for them because that took more strength to speak then than I had at that point. The boys got up and told stories that Blake wrote or things they had written. They did a wonderful job and even those of us too sad to laugh had to smile at the memories they had. Our cousin Chris and I did the readings. Then it was the priest' turn. When I say this man spoke for what felt like HOURS about a man and a fish, even my Grandma had had enough. We all joke now that he had never seen his church so full and decided that now was a good time to try and give all his Sunday sermons into one. It went on forever and when he finally stepped down from the podium, I was shocked when the crowd didn't applaud that it was finally over.

Afterward, we all left to go to the KC home where Scott's side of the family had made sure we had gumbo and potato salad for everyone. To this day, I'm not sure who paid for the food, the KC home, or even cooked it all, but I know Scott's family had it taken care of and I could not be more thankful to them for that. We had a toolbox from someone's truck that we propped up for people to put mementos in to send down to Blake the next day. Our racing friends had brought a checkered flag for everyone to sign and send down.

256

We all sat and ate and enjoyed the company. More stories came but a few less tears. Now it was time to celebrate as Blake would have wanted us to. There's a song that came out not too long after that titled "Here for a Good Time" by George Strait, Blake was always up for a good time and now it was time we started having one too. Daniel and I hopped in Blake's truck and headed south to Fourchon. We jammed out to rock and roll music with the windows down the whole way. I finally felt like my job was over and now I could grieve. I could get drunk. I could have a nervous breakdown. I could do whatever it took to make the pain bearable because now I could finally sit back and let myself feel it. I could get mad at Blake for leaving me here and in charge because had it been anyone else, it would have been him in charge instead. He was the one who took over when things got tough and it wasn't a job I wanted. Now that his services were over, it wasn't a job I could do anymore. So I jammed out to music and decided, I was going to party with everyone else. Daniel needed the music as bad as I did. He hadn't stopped to grieve either because he knew he couldn't lose it or I was done. I relied on him so much that week and he stood strong the whole time. I'll never know what that took for him to put aside his own feelings to keep me sane, but I'll spend the rest of my life trying to be there for him. We held hands and cried and sang and laughed because the truck seemed to want to pull into every gas station because we hadn't gotten beer iced down yet. The truck knew his owner well enough to know there should be beer here.

Friday night, everyone went to Nobile's camp. More stories, more tears, and more toasts to Blake went around. The boys also had to get the toolbox ready for sinking, which meant a fun paint job, some weights, and a lot of holes needed to be done. The guys had fun painting skulls and cross bones and other silly things on the box. The items that went into it actually had a good amount of weight, but I

257

think some bricks and cinder blocks were added for good measure. Then the holes had to be created. The men began to try and drill holes but either the toolbox was that strong or the drill was that weak because all it did was create some dents. Finally, people started taking out some of their anger on the box. Back side of a hammer seemed to work pretty well for creating a hole when hit hard enough. I tried, and even with all of my anger with Blake for making me plan his funeral and write his obituary, I wasn't strong enough to create any holes so I let Daniel make them for me.

After a while, it was just a group of extended family sitting around drinking and having a good time. Then we all piled up into Blake's truck to head back to the camp we were staying at, with most of the heavy partiers riding in the bed. As soon as we pull up, the people in the bed insist that we need some food. With everything that had gone on that day, not many of us had stopped to eat. Someone goes inside and heats up some corn dogs. Chad, my cousin ate his corn dog and would not stop talking about how it was the best corn dog EVER! The pure happiness on his face when he discovered that we had more if he wanted some. He has yet to live that one down.

Saturday morning was not easy to wake up for. The boats going to the rig were leaving at dawn and most of us had just gone to bed somewhere around 4 or 5. Alarms were ignored but we eventually drug ourselves up and drove over to Craig's camp where all the boats were meeting up. Luckily, the people in charge of getting the boats ready drank as much as us the night before so they were also running late. Some of us immediately curled up in whatever spot we could find to catch a little more sleep. Around 7:30, around 10 boats headed out with the original Skanktuary in the lead. Each boat had their Jolly Roger flags flying and the weather was perfect for the ride 70 miles offshore to Lobster 873A. The water was calm enough that the guys could have brought out their wakeboards. When we arrived at the rig, the boats all began to circle around with flags flying high like we were celebrating the winning of a race. The guys on the rig had no clue what was going on but they cheered us since obviously someone was having a good time and I'm sure they wished they could be a part of it. Eventually, with all the boats causing havoc on the water below, the rig shut down production for the day and let us play without any of the noise. Everyone hopped in the water and swam from boat to boat just in awe of this beautiful place that most of us would have never seen had Blake not made this his final resting place. Mom and Rachel stayed behind, Rachel being pregnant, and Mom just not ready to see this spot yet. Scott however, had taken the ride out. I knew this was his first time seeing the rig and since we rode up on different boats, I sought him out immediately. The grief on his face when I saw him was something I won't forget. Dustin must have needed to find Scott as well because he had swam up not two minutes later.

Boats at Blake's Memorial

Eventually we gathered the boats together and began to do the service on the water. The last gifts were given in the toolbox and then the guys locked it up. Dad said some words, as did Dustin, Jr., Jared, Nobile, and myself. I hardly remember what I said, much less anyone else, but needless to say, there were many tears. We all poured a beer into the water and sent the toolbox to the bottom as someone cranked up "For Those About to Rock" by AC/DC. Someone said there were around 140 people out there. Two hours offshore, in water 900 feet deep where nearly a dozen boats, each one filled to capacity and all, with tears in their eyes, saluted to Captain BT. It was an unforgettable moment. Not long after, Jr. stood up on the tallest part of the boat he could find to let everyone know that we had officially drank every ounce of our 50 cases of beer and that we needed to head in.

All of the smoke bombs had been set off as well as the flares. There were many sunglasses in Blake's favorite brand that were lost as well as a prop, a few watches, and some chains. We joked that Blake not only was set with beer, but he insisted on making sure he had a few accessories as well. We all headed in to the Baudoin's camp. If there were 140 people out on the water, the camp had to have at least double that many people. There was food and beer for all. We drank and danced around. We put on Jimmy Buffet's "A Pirates Look at Forty" for the first time and everyone realized just how fitting the song actually was. We all gathered on the dock and Mom said a few words for the first time. Even in her shock, she found the right words to set everyone at ease. While we all knew there would be outrageous hurdles ahead in growing to accept his death, she did a great job of getting people started. We dropped all of our flowers in the water and watched as they slowly floated out to Blake.

Not long after Blake's death, we discovered that I was pregnant with our first child. We had decided to start trying, but with everything going on, we simply forgot. Although a lot of people think it, I don't believe in any way that Blake sent some spiritual influence to make me conceive. Blake simply would have pretended that any pregnancy of mine was another Virgin Mary occurrence and stuck with that. However, I do realize that I prayed simply to feel happy again. While everyone else was in their own world of grief, Daniel and I had something to feel excited about. Cameron was born in May and from his first day, he was the happiest baby I have ever seen. He would smile at you to just to see if you would smile back. I asked to feel happy, so happiness was sent to me in this little bundle of joy. I hate that Cameron will never know his uncle by anything more than a name, but that's life. There's not a day that goes by that I don't miss Blake. I still look around at family gatherings and think "Who's missing? Oh yea, Blake." The tears still come just as hard and the grief is just as strong, but it's fewer and farther between than it once was. After tragedies happen, you just want to get back to normal, but what no one tells you is that there is no more normal. Your life as you know it has changed forever. Sooner or later, you find your new normal, but it will always include that feeling of loss. People eventually start saying hello again instead of running away from you in fear of saying the wrong thing. One day you realize that you've gone through the whole day without feeling so bad. You almost feel guilty because it feels like life is moving on and that life shouldn't move on without him. The next day might not be so easy, but the good days begin to beat out the bad. I feel so lucky to have grown up with the family I have. I was as close with my siblings as anyone could hope to be and I loved being a part of what other people just called "those crazy Terry kids." I admittedly didn't do much to help the crazy part of our reputation, but I was always happy to go along for the ride. I had 24 years of my life with my older brother and I have no regrets. Not only do I know my brother loved me and he knew how much I loved him, I also know my brother and I were friends. We didn't just tolerate each other because we were family; we liked hanging out and enjoyed ragging each other about anything and everything. So few people are lucky enough to have what I did. Because of that, I will do all that I can to make sure my children have that same closeness. The things he taught me are a part of me and will be a part of my family. So I may not be able to talk to Blake or give him a hug, but when I look at all of our children playing together, I can smile realizing that he will never truly be gone.

Dustin, Whitney and Blake in St. Lucia

"I am hard pressed between the two. My desire is to depart and be with Christ, for that is far better. But to remain in the flesh is more necessary on your account." Philippians 1:23-24

Chapter 47

Johnny's Camp

By Cindie Roussel and Johnny Pinell

"I wonder if he has a key on this key chain." Daniel said as he tried to open the door. "Check this out, first key I put in the door." Daniel turns the knob and opens the door for me to walk in. Blake had this huge key ring full of keys. Most were keys from different one's camps between Fourchon and Grand Isle. Of course, the first key Daniel tries out, fits the door to Johnny's camp.

I look around as the camp is dark with the curtains drawn. The smell of the room is musty as it seemed to have been locked up for a while. Probably since Blake had been there last. There are fishing rods in the corner with a couple of bean bag chairs next to them. There is a leather sofa and chair worn from sitting and a lamp with fishing lures hanging off of it. As I look to the left, there is a long hall leading to the bedrooms. "So this is it," I thought to myself. "This is Johnny's camp. This is the place that my baby stayed when he was not home with us." I walked to the curtains and I pulled them open to let in what sunlight was left from a long day traveling down to Fourchon. I looked down at the boat harbor and there sat Johnny's boat. On the dock was a swing hanging from the covered platform about 15 feet high. Blake built that swing as he loved to sit outside and look at the evening sun go down. Next to the swing was a fish station for cutting and filleting fish. He had an ice machine put in to make sure he could always ice down the catch of the day. "So much work gone to waste, Blake built all of this and he is not here to enjoy these things." I thought. Then I turned and started to walk down the hallway. I ran my hand over the wall as I was hoping to feel something…anything. When I reached the bathroom on the left, I saw Blake's hat on the top of the cabinet. I reached for it and pulled it to my chest. I burst into tears as this was the first time I felt that Blake was never coming back to me. He was gone. Here I am sitting in the camp he loved so much for the very first time. The camp he put his heart and soul in building to make it a warm home and he was gone! I looked around and all I could see was Blake's home. He had made Johnny's camp his home.

When Johnny offered his camp for my family to stay during Blake's celebration of life, I had no idea what to expect. I had only been down to Fourchon and Grand Isle at Easter so I had never visited Johnny's camp. I was overwhelmed at how his camp had so much of Blake's spirit in it, that by the end of the weekend, we started calling Johnny's camp, "Blake's camp." We even wrote down Blake's Rules for staying at his camp on a paper plate.

Blake's Camp Rules:
No shirt, no shoes are allowed
No complaining
No curling irons
No hair spray
No ironing clothes

…silly things like that. It was something we could hear Blake say if we were all together. Then reality would set in, we were all together, but Blake was missing.

Johnny shares his story of how Blake and he met for the very first time.

Johnny's Camp

My memory of Blake's first time diving was when Toby Boudreaux, Albert Pinell and I were at my camp. I have a camp in Fourchon and a 36' Contender. Well we were leaving to go out in the morning and Jesse and Blake showed up, drinking of course. Jesse would come pretty often with me fishing offshore but this would be Blake's first time. Finally we got to leave and it was a beautiful day to be out in the gulf. Toby and I both scuba dive so we both dove a lot of times on the way offshore. We would free dive around the satellite platforms for lemon fish. Both Toby and I jumped in and shot a fish. Blake wanted to try it so he strips down to his underwear, puts on a mask, snorkel and fins and jumps in. Well from that point on he was hooked. Within two months he was certified to dive. After that it was what he lived for. The camp became "BT's Camp" and he became "The Captain" of my boat. He would have everything ready to go when we went there. He took advantage of every opportunity he had to dive.

Johnny and Blake

Johnny and Blake became best of friends and they spent a lot of time on the water. Johnny meant the world to Blake. I can remember one evening Blake came in the back door with a pale look on his face. I asked him what was wrong, but he just shrugged his shoulders and said, "Nothing." He fixed a plate of food from the stove and sat down at the kitchen table, as he had done so many nights. I was standing at the sink when he dropped his fork in his plate and he started to cry. I dropped what I was doing, put my arms around him and I asked, "Baby, what is wrong." He said, "Mah, I almost lost Johnny today." "What happened?" I replied. "We were diving together and I thought he was coming up with me when I realized he was on the bottom. He was not moving. We were both about out of air and he was below 250 feet. I knew that we both were in trouble but I had to get to him. I almost blacked out but I was able to get us both to the top. I have never dove that deep, but I was so scared of losing him. I almost lost him today, Mah! I almost lost him!"

I will never forget us sitting at the table as he could not stop crying. He loved Johnny with all his heart and he feared the thought of losing him. I can remember Nobile walking up my walkway to our house with Blake's bag from the boat. His parents standing in the drive way in disbelief. No one knew what to do. Nobile's face was pale and I could tell he was in shock. Here this young man lived through what Blake feared. They were best friends just like Johnny and Blake. They spent night after night working together on the Skank so she would be ready by the weekends. Nobile suffered so much and none of us will ever know that pain he felt that day. Blake loved Nobile like he loved Johnny and the last thing he ever wanted to do was put Nobile through any kind of pain. When Blake wrote the Hemingway Code Hero back in college, he wrote, "Facing death is the only way a Hero may face himself." I question if he knew his fate? Did he write these words about himself or for those he left behind?

Johnny told me that he wanted to sell the camp when Blake died. I felt the same way. Everything that we built together seem to be a waste to me. But Johnny's camp was different. It was Blake's haven that he loved and spent his every spare moment he had at his camp. All the modifications Blake made were those he felt were important. Blake was so much like his Grandpa Chester. If we were to have crawfish every Friday night at the shop, we needed beer. So Chester had the boys modify a refrigerator for a keg. Blake had all his things he needed for a weekend of fishing at Johnny's camp. He built the fish stand with the ice machine. He built that beautiful swing that hung 15 feet from the pavilion. All these things were essential for the camp in Blake's eyes.

As I sat in that very same swing Blake built, I looked at Johnny and said, "You can't sell your camp. It's all we have left of Blake and he built all these things for us to enjoy."

"I expect to pass through life but
once. If, therefore, there be any
kindness I can show, or any good
thing I can do for any fellow being,
let me do it now ... as I shall not
pass this way again."
William Penn

Chapter 48

RIG 873

By Cindie Roussel

My children decided to throw me a surprised 50th birthday party this year although I really did not want any type of celebration. It just did not seem right to me to celebrate without Blake being here. He was one to always come up with surprises or funny jokes and without him, it just did not seem right. He loved to play jokes on me especially on April 1st. He loved April fools jokes and no matter how prepared I would be for something, he always got me.

Whitney planned my party with Rachel, Katy, Dustin, Daniel and Scott's help. She is so much like me and she knows what I like. Tables must be round and should be covered in linen with beautiful centerpieces. Beautiful decorations along with making sure the food is perfect so that the party guest will remember how delicious it was. Invitations must be sent out in a timely manner as to making sure all the guests are prepared to attend. Planning is so important, especially when you are the hostess and you want to make sure everything is perfect.

Whitney was so prepared that she wanted me to be prepared for my day. She made sure to buy me a dress so that I was not underdressed for the occasion. However, this was a clue for me that something was up as Scott tried to convince me that he bought me a dress to take me to dinner. Now, Scott is not one to go shopping, let alone buy me a dress. He may be able to pick out a fishing shirt or a hat that he thinks I might like, but a dress?

He had a diversion planned as we had planned to go to dinner and my girlfriend Debbie called me for us to meet her and her husband, Jacque for drinks. Debbie had been diagnosed with breast cancer two years prior and she finally had her reconstructive surgery. She was celebrating her new boob job, yes her one new boob replacement. She wanted to celebrate, so of course, we said yes. She asked us to meet her at a local bar and restaurant in Houma.

When we arrived around 6:30, I thought, "This is kind of early to be meeting for drinks, but its Debbie and she is wanting to have some fun, so why not." As we turned the corner into the hallway, the doors were open and everyone shouted, "Surprise!" Startled, I jumped back and then realized I knew everyone. The faces were so warm and so full of smiles. There in the room were the children I told stories to in Church, my minister, Glenda; there were new friends and old friends; there were family and co-workers all standing there with smiles. There were friends I had not seen in several years. There were my children and grandchildren smiling as I cried and embraced them all.

At that moment, all I could remember was that I felt like I was walking through the gates of heaven. I often wonder on the day that Blake died, did he know he was going to die. Did he have a clue that Jesus was planning his special day to be that day at that platform, Rig 873 where he was diving? Did he have any clue that there was a surprise waiting for him on the other side and that Jesus was there waiting for him? Was he greeted by the warm faces of family and friends? Is that what heaven will be when we all meet Jesus at the gates of heaven?

Scott and Me (My birthday party)

The weekend Blake died, he was supposed to go to the red dress run in New Orleans with Jr., but last minute he was diverted by an invitation to go fishing. That Thursday before they left out, Blake and Nobile had stopped at my office to see me before they left. Blake never stopped by work as he would call me instead, but that day for some reason he stopped by. He told me how excited he was to be going on the boat and that he could not wait. As both of them were running out the door, I yelled at them to please be careful. Nobile hollered back, "If we're not back home by Sunday, call the Coast Guard." I will never forget how they both were full speed anxious to be down in Fourchon.

The following Saturday, things were quiet. Scott was fishing for the first time in a long time and I was working around the house. I just poured myself a glass of wine when the phone rang. It was Jared asking if I had heard from Blake. Within minutes of hanging up the phone with Jared, the next call was Nobile. My life fell apart within seconds of a phone call. I called Scott next. "Where are you?" I asked. "Just picked up the boat heading home right now." he said. "It's Blake, he did not surface" as I could not believe the words coming out of my mouth. "He made a dive and he did not surface!" I started to cry. "Oh God, I am on my way." He said.

I called Dustin next. I don't remember what I said. Necole, my neighbor called Whitney. Whitney called Tony and Tony called me. I can remember Tony saying, "I am numb. I don't know what to do? I am so numb." Then I knew I had to call Rachel. "Rachel, is anyone with you?" I asked. She said, "No, why?" "Rachel, Blake did not surface after he made a dive today." "What? What do you mean?" her voice now shaking. "Rachel, can you call someone to bring you here?" I asked. "Yes." I could tell she was in shock as I was in disbelief as I had to tell her this horrible news.

The last call I remember making was to my sister, Kathie. At this point, the words were rehearsed, "Blake did not surface." I kept repeating over and over, but I did not believe what I was saying. She could tell that I was in a state of shock. "I'm on my way." she said. The calls after that started pouring in. I felt like this was a nightmare and I could not wake up. Something must have happened and he is probably on the rig. He has had close encounters before, but he always came out of them, I hoped.

Jared and Nikki were one of the first to arrive. Jared grabbed me as tight as he could and then told me that he was headed down to help put together a team of divers. The last words I said to Jared, "Bring my baby home, PLEASE JARED, BRING HIM HOME!"

Slowly, friends and family piled in one by one. Our house was full of love and support from so many. There were friends I had not seen in years. Kid's that grew up with Blake, all piling in. Brenda, my longtime best friend, just wrapped her arms around me. Here the two of us had 34 years together through thick and thin, but nothing prepared us for this. We had just spent the beginning of the year together celebrating Whitney's wedding. Such a happy time and never had clue that our world was going to fall apart 5 months later.

Kathie tried to keep me sedated as I was hurting so bad that she wanted to do whatever she could to stop the pain. Nothing, I mean NOTHING can relieve that emptiness of losing a child.
The night grew heavy as the waiting by the phone was hell. Rachel and Dustin arrived and then Whitney and Daniel. We all held each other crying. Dustin said, "Mah, we'll find him, I promise." They all headed down to Fourchon to join Tony and others. Boats were being lined up and these young men were putting together teams of divers as we had no clue that the Coast Guard was not going to dive searching for Blake. They used night vision equipment and helicopters searching for signs of movement, but no diving equipment or ROVs to search below the surface. Blake was at a 900' platform, the odds of rescue or recovery was getting slim.

Then a call comes in from Lauren Slowick, Blake's old high school sweetheart, that she had talked to the Coast Guard and that someone had reported seeing a diver's tank floating in the water. For one split second, we all had hope. Everyone was running around the house with excitement that maybe they had found him. Quickly, the hope deteriorated when it was not a tank that matched Blake's.

The next morning, the sun came up but it was dark inside my head. People were everywhere. Sleeping on anything they could lay their bodies.

I stood by the coffee pot and started screaming again, "God, why are you punishing me? I have been so faithful, why would you take my baby? Why, OH GOD, WHY?" I screamed. Kathie and Glenda, my minister both grabbed me and started trying to comfort me, but nothing helped.

Most of the day, I lay in bed holding a pillow to my stomach and I could not stop the tears. Every time the phone would ring, I jumped and ran as fast as I could to only hear no words of hope. At one moment, one of the girls phone received a text message, **"COAST GUARD CALLED OFF THE SEARCH."** I went screaming through the house! Everyone chasing me to try to calm me down and I just fell to my knees and curled up in a ball crying. That evening, the Coast Guard called to tell me that they had called off the search, but would keep the cutter in the area.

The next thing I knew was that Tony was getting an ROV and those young men were not giving up. They made several dives and continued to try with the ROV, but ran into a lot of troubles with the equipment.

Dustin finally called late Monday night, "Mah, we can keep searching. We will not stop unless you tell us." He said. "Dustin, come home." The words fell from my lips without hesitation. It was as though someone was in control of my body and talking for me. I asked him to let me speak to Jr. He handed Jr. the phone. "Jr., come home." I told him. Tears in his voice, he said, "I don't want to leave him here." I said, "I know, Blake does not want to be found. It's time to come home. I need you." "Okay." He replied.

Blake (last pictures of him)

The pictures in this chapter are ones that we have never shared with anyone as these were the last pictures of Blake just before he died. In these pictures, I look deep into his eyes to see if I can tell if he had a clue. He seemed to be looking off at the rig as though something was drawing him.

Nobile told me that they were tired and he really did not want to make another dive, but Blake was persistent so he agreed. Something must have drawn Blake to make that last dive. Someone was speaking to him in his heart.

Rig 873 is not where Blake is now, but it is the place where Blake entered the gates of heaven. At that moment that he drew his last breath, he saw Jesus standing there with his arms open wide. Jesus was the host and he had prepared for his coming.

Blake
(This is the very last photo taken before he made his final dive)

He had the tables covered in linens with the beautiful centerpieces. He had prepared the feast and all the guests were there. There was Grandpa Chester with his big smile so happy to finally have Blake with him again. There was Aunt Rose and Uncle Bradley, smiling for him to come and sit down at the table full of crawfish. There was Papa Art and Aunt Celeste, Scott's sister, who could not wait to hear another one of Blake's funny stories. There was my brother, Thomas who could not wait to show him the city of gold. There was Tre' who could not wait to show him the best places to fish and ski.

The guests were all there, with arms open wide and warm faces full of smiles. Blake was fully dressed in white linens as Jesus placed his arms around him. At that moment, I know in my heart, Blake embraced Jesus as I did my children that day of my birthday party. He was full of happiness and love. He knew at that moment, he was crossing the gates of heaven. At that same time, seven men on that boat had to say goodbye. Those seven men had to come back home without their friend. I can't imagine what they felt as they slowly traveled back to shore. Is this how the apostles felt the night they had to tell Jesus goodbye? I believe that they were in shock because they did not understand why Jesus had to die. Like Jesus, we don't understand why Blake had to die.

After a few weeks, Nikki called me to tell me that Jared had a gift that he wanted to bring to me and if it would be okay if they stop by later that evening. I said sure. When they arrived, Jared handed me a small squared stained box shaped like a treasure box. Inside the box was an Oyster sponge that he had pulled off the rig the night he dove to try to recovery Blake. He said that he knew after the second dive, they were not going to find him and he had promised me that he would bring him home. He was so at a loss but he knew he had to bring me something back. I remember the first thought I had was at least this was something. We had nothing when Blake was lost. No trace of anything. No shirt, no mask, no tank, nothing. This was something.

**An Oyster Sponge from Rig 873 where Blake made his last
dive**

Now, I sit and look at this beautiful gift and I feel so grateful. This
oyster sponge was there with Blake when he entered the gates of
heaven and how this tiny gift is the closest thing to heaven that I will
ever have. How God must have spoken to Jared to tell him to bring
me something back, anything that would give me some peace. No,
Blake is not there at Rig 873. He entered God's kingdom through
the gates of Heaven at Rig 873.

Chapter 49

A Hidden Treasure

By Cindie Roussel

When Nobile brought me Blake's bag from the boat, I put it up in the closet as I just could not bring myself to open it. He also brought back all his dive gear and his favorite spear gun, "The Black Pearl." Blake had named his spear gun, the Black Pearl. He always had a nickname for something and why should his spear gun be any different. The odd thing to me was that he did not have this particular gun with him when he went down. He was using a different one for some reason. His gun is short with a long steel shaft and black frame. Why he named her the Black Pearl, I am not sure. To a Pirate, pearls are like a hidden treasure. They are born from oysters complete with a shimmering iridescence, luster and soft inner glow unlike any other gem on earth. Pearls are grown by live oysters far below the surface of the sea. Unlike Pearls, Gemstones must be cut and polished to bring out their beauty. But pearls do not require any treatment to reveal their loveliness. Blake had an inner beauty that was given by God. He was given to all of us to realize how important God's love is and to show us how we are to live our lives.

As soon as we realized Blake was not coming home, I just went with the flow as I was numb and I could not grasp reality at this point. When we called off the search, everyone headed back home from Fourchon. Tony came through the door hollering my name. I can remember him holding me telling me that he was so sorry he could not bring him home. One by one, they came through the door. Dustin and Jr. finally arrived and I asked them to all sit with me in the living room. "I can't do this alone. I need all of you to help me give Blake the service that he would want. I will not do this right, so I need your help." I said while trying to compose myself. I knew at that moment, I had to pull myself together to make sure they all stayed strong. The next few days getting ready for the memorial services, I was in shock. That was probably the best word to describe me. Whitney took care of everything, although I just don't know how. Our house was full of kids putting together pictures for the church. We had laptops, printers and cell phones everywhere. Hanna, Tina's other daughter had developed the pictures for his memorial to go on the bulletin boards. I can remember her face as she walked in the door. She could not say a word but just wrapped her arms around me as she balled her eyes out. Donnie, Necole's husband was cooking tons of food as he did not know what to do but to try to keep busy. Tyler and Samantha, their children just kept bringing food over to the house. No one knew what to do but just go with the flow.

Scott, Whitney, Rachel and I headed to the church to make preparations. I can remember Rachel almost losing it between the Priest and the newspapers not cooperating with us. The Priest wanted things his way and the newspapers would not print the obituary without a death certificate. Little did we know this was the beginning of a nightmare of not being able to name Blake Jr. or being able to claim social security benefits for him.

That morning of Blake's service, I was just there. Not in mind but in body. We prepared for the people to arrive. And they did...the line of people was beyond belief. They just kept coming. It became obvious to me that we had to take care of the people as the hurt and loss that we all had felt was pouring into the church. I can remember telling Kathie to hold the line so I could go to the restroom as I wanted to comfort everyone coming through the door. I can remember the hot bodies as they stood outside the doors in lines in the hot sun. I started moving myself to the back of the line as I wanted to assure all of them that it was going to be okay. "Blake was where we all ultimately want to be," I repeated this phrase to comfort each one that came through the door. At one point, Whitney told me that we will have to extend the service one hour as the lines were still outside at 12:00. The priest announced that we would move the service back one hour and that the police were outside as the traffic had backed up outside due to the people pouring through the door. We as a family were overwhelmed with emotion as we had no idea the people Blake had touched. All walks of life came through those church doors that day. I can only tell you that at that moment did I realize this was bigger than us. Blake's legacy is more than being my son or Hank's father or best friend but that he is God's son who he was given the Grace to move and touch others in a way that only God could provide.

After Blake's Memorial, so many cards and letters came in that I could not find myself to want to read them. Believe it or not, I guess I thought if I did not open them then it was not real. Blake was not gone and this was all just a nightmare that I would eventually wake up to the life I knew before. But the days turned into weeks and the weeks into months until finally I decided to start reading some of the letters. As I read them, I realized how he touched so many lives. One particular letter that touched me was from Tony Guilbeau's mother, Maloy Guilbeau. I had never met her but I knew her son, Tony and Blake were very close friends. She not only wrote to me, but to each of my children. I thought this was so beautiful for someone to take the time to write to each of us. I knew her hurt was deep and she was reaching out to each of us to try to comfort us. Blake had to have been so special to her. Here is one of her letters:

Cindie and Scott,
I have to say thank you for raising such a great son...Blake really became a soul in our family. We spent so much time with him at our camp in Grand Isle. He had the biggest heart and sweetest smile, always happy and willing to help

out…his life made a difference in so many lives and he will never be forgotten. He was a person who was always encouraging never down. He had so many good traits the he would do anything for his friends. His life was short but he left a very good impact on those he was around. Blake loved life to the highest. He was such a blessing to our family. He will be missed deeply. Sincerely, Maloy.

Her letters touched me so much. It was evident through her messages that Blake had that inner beauty that Maloy loved about him. He was real and he had made a difference in not only her life but others. I don't think any of us knew how much until that morning of his memorial. All the rough times and me worried if he was ever going to settle down from his wild adventurous life. Never did it dawn on me that he was living the right life all along. He was doing God's work by touching so many lives. Blake was that hidden treasure I never knew until that very morning.

O that Pearl of great price! Have you found it?
Is the Savior supreme in your love?
O consider it well, ere you answer.
As you hope for a welcome above.
Have you given up all for this Treasure?
Have you counted past gains as but loss?
Has your trust in yourself and your merits
Come to naught before Christ and His Cross?

The Swedish hymn Den Kostiliga Parlan (O That Pearl of Great Price!)

Matthew 13:44, 46 states "The kingdom of heaven is like treasure hidden in a field. When a man found it, he hid it again, and then in his joy went and sold all he had and bought that field. "Again, the kingdom of heaven is like a merchant looking for fine pearls. When he found one of great value, he went away and sold everything he had and bought it.

This past Christmas, Scott gave me a Tahitian Black Pearl in memory of Blake.

Chapter 50

Lockup Your Daughters and Wives

By Cindie Roussel

When Blake reached the age of nine, he started to question about the "facts of life." He wanted to know when it would be his time to have sex. Can you imagine at the age of 9? I was stunned to think he needed to know about sex this early in his life, however Blake was the curious one and he was not stopping until he got the answers he was looking for. So, the next day I went to the local drug store and bought a box of condoms. That evening, we sat down after supper to begin our discussion about "when will he know it is his time to have sex." I told him that a man and woman fall in love and get married and then they have sex. He did not buy into that one at all. So I then said that if he could not wait to get married before having sex, that he should practice safe sex. Safe sex at nine years old, are you kidding me? Anyways, I pulled out one of the condoms and rolled it out to show him. Now visualize a mother sitting at the kitchen table showing her son how a condom works. Can you see it? Rolling out this extra large size condom to a nine year old telling him that this has to go, you know? It has to go there? As I rolled out the condom, I could see relief in Blake's face. Once he saw the size of the condom, he said, "Whew, I got a while before I can wear one of those." And that was it! He was satisfied that he had time before he would ever have to wear a condom. Looking back now, he just wanted reassurance that he had time before reaching that next level in his life.

Blake in his younger days at the Lockport Parade

Blake was always open to talking with me about sex, and just about anything, I think. He was honest and sometimes too open about his life to me, but I am grateful for that now. He had many women that he admired, but a select few that he really loved. Each had a bond with him that kept them close, no matter whether they dated or whether they were best friends, they had a bond no doubt. This was evident at his funeral as each arrived full of tears and sorrow. It was amazing to me that each had such fond memories with him, that I am grateful that they remembered only the good times and the friendship that they shared.

~Sara~

Blake and Sara

It all started with a little girl across the street named Sara. She was four years old and Blake was three. They did everything together. If she had gum, he had to have gum. If she had a pool, he had to have a pool. If she got a bike, he had to have a bike. Well one day coming home, Blake saw Sara riding her bike in the drive way. It was

289

devastating to him to see her riding WITHOUT training wheels. His face became swollen as she hollered, "Blake, look at me, no training wheels!" He marched inside the house and he was mad. I told him that we could go outside and practice, but he would not hear of it. He was not going to let her see him practice. So that night, we practiced up and down our hallway. We had tire marks and handlebar scrapes that it looked like someone destroyed our hallway with a black marks-a-lot. It was pretty bad, but he did it. The very next day, he was cruising with Sara as he was not going to let her get the best of him. I think at that moment, I knew Blake loved the ladies and he was always going to try to impress them, but never let them get the best of him.

Sara and Blake grew apart as time and distance does that to us all. I was able to find Sara by contacting her mother, Barbara over the web. I just felt this chapter was not complete without Sara. Here is what she had to tell me:

"I have fond memories of my friendship with Blake as well my relationship with you and your family. My mom and I often reflect back to our Linda Circle days and with those memories always to our time with you all. I cannot even begin to imagine what you and your family have experienced. As a mother, I strongly admire your enthusiasm in sharing Blake's life and carrying out his goodness. After reading this chapter, I can see what a fine man Blake grew to be. I always knew this was the case, even at such a young age. But as time and distance grew between us, I always wondered where life took him. Thank you for sharing this chapter with me. I am anxious to read the entire book!" "Thank you," Sara.

Lockup Your Daughters and Wives

~Whitney~

Blake and Whitney

Blake and Whitney had the typical sister and brother relationship like most sisters and brothers, I believe. However Whitney and Dustin are only a year apart so when it came to arguments in the house, they both ganged up on Blake. When Jessica and Allison, their step-sisters joined the family, it became an army against Blake. Blake was the oldest and he always felt as though he was responsible for all of them. I don't know if this was just in his nature or if it was my fault as Tony and I separated when Blake was five and I would always tell him that he was the man of the house now. That was a lot of pressure I had put on him not realizing that maybe this would affect him later in life. As both Whitney and Dustin got older, he watched over them and he made sure they stayed out of trouble. When it came to Whitney, Blake could see right through her. She could tell a lie and I could never see it, but he could. He would say, "Mah, she's lying, you can't see it?" Not that Whit told many lies but back then, she was a bit sneaky and I had no clue. As for the boys, I always knew as for some reason they just could never get away with anything.

As Whitney got older, I saw a change in their relationship. Blake became more protective of her as Whitney started to become noticeable to the boys. When she would bring a boy to the house, both Blake and Dustin made sure to be there to meet him. It was a wonder she could date at all, but those she did date, they knew where they stood with her brothers. Not to mention, Blake's friends started to notice her and he made sure they knew she was off-limits!

When Whitney met Daniel, she had met Blake's match. Daniel and Blake had so much in common. They handled things the same way. If you had a problem, you duke it out and then you sit down and have a drink over it. The first time Blake met Daniel, he told that exact thing to Daniel. He said, "Daniel, we might not see eye to eye and we may end up in the back yard fighting over it, but we will then come back and sit down and have a drink together because we have to get along. Whitney loves you and that's the way things have to be."

Blake, Daniel, Whitney and Dustin

The Famous Speech
"I always let lil' brother take care of Whitney. If I had to get involved...BAD NEWS!"

:

~Jessica~

One of my favorite and most memorable stories of Blake involved some toys I have gotten that summer; Furbies. These were the toys who spoke a different language, you had to feed, and just interacted with anyone who came by. One day, Allison, Whitney, Dustin and I were in the kitchen doing something when Blake walked into the living room where the Furbies were placed. He walked by them and triggered the motion sensor so of course they started chatting away. I remember Blake just looking at them then looking around then back to them with this utter look of confusion. The important thing to note about Furbies was that they did not stop talking unless you fed them or took the batteries out. Well, they continue to talk and instead of walking away, Blake proceeds to have a conversation with them for the next few minutes. The rest of us just sat in the kitchen watching this hilarious display of toy interaction. Finally we decide to help Blake out when we couldn't keep our laughs quiet anymore and turn off the Furbies. This furbie story is a memory I will always remember especially now that the Furbie is back on the shelves.

The first few months after I met Blake I remember him clearly wanting nothing to do with me. I was the annoying 9 year old girl and he was the super cool 15 year old boy who had way too much to do then entertain me. Blake used to be put in charge of babysitting me, AKA leaving me alone while he and his friend snuck out to go the movies, and of course I always tattled on him every single time he did it to which he would usually throw me on the ground or picked on me or put peanut butter in my sleeping bag. Well one day we all went on a boat ride in the Gulf. The boat actually broke down mid ride so we all stopped on a small beach while the guys fixed it. While waiting, all of us girls decided to go swimming even to the warning of the strong current. At this time, Blake wasn't fixing the boat or swimming; instead he was making boobs out of the sand on the beach. Well, we are all just floating along when we realize that the beach is getting much farther away and it was getting very hard to swim back. I have a life jacket on but being only 9 this current was doing a number on me. Then out of nowhere here comes Blake to my rescue. He brought a boogie board, loaded me on it, and brought me back to shore. That moment made me realize that even though he picked on me and I tattled on him I guess this is what it was like to have a big brother, someone who would take time out of making their boob sand castle to come rescue me from floating out to sea.

The summer Blake lived with us in Illinois is one big story in itself. I had for one never lived with a boy growing up and quickly learned that boys eat a lot and eat all the time. Plus this was also when he was really into those protein shakes and those tubs were everywhere. That summer I met numerous "girlfriends" and every single one of them was so in love with Blake and his charm. He also taught me to never get drunk pass out then have someone put you in the truck with the windows rolled down and no keys; rain makes for an unfortunate wake up call. That 4th of July, Blake demonstrated what happens when you get hit by a fire work that spins. It turns you shirt chest red and you scream like a little girl.

While that summer did have some ups and downs, it's that summer that I learned what it was like to have an older brother and it was the best experience. From playing video games late at night, throwing me in the lake fully clothed, wrestling in the kitchen, listening to my day, watching unsolved mysteries, trying to understand what he was actually saying, not telling mom how he had a snake in the basement, having all his "girlfriends" tell me how much they loved him, and how he watched me walk down the street one night so nobody would get me; that summer is one I will never forget.

Dustin, Whitney, Jessica, Allison and Blake

~Allison~

Blake was the one who taught me to let loose and chill. He was always encouraging and supportive of my "nerdy" ways. One of my favorite memories with Blake was when I had just turned 18 and he was in Texas visiting, he talked me into going out one night. I had only been out a few times before so I had no clue what to expect with Blake. As soon as we got to the country bar, we made our way to the bar and Blake soon charmed an older lady into buying drinks for not only him but me as well. He then proceeded to mingle with a large group of middle-aged women and who taught him to dance the two-step. Once he was an expert, as he then deemed himself to be after 10 minutes of practice, we hit the dance floor and two-stepped for the rest of the night. We ended up having a great time and we both enjoyed our first time in a true Texas country bar. Now, every time I go out to a country bar I am reminded of that night. It was just us and although we saw each other often, it was the first time we truly spent a lot of time together without our other siblings and parents around.

Dustin, Allison, Jessica, Whitney and Blake

~Candace~

Candace is my sister, Kathie's youngest child. Blake and Candace were so close in age that I can remember the two of them fighting. Blake was the typical rough boy and Candace was the "Ms. Princess."

Candace and Blake

As the years passed by and they both reached that maturity age, they became the best of friends. They were more like brother and sister then cousins. Blake loved Candace with his whole heart and he would do anything to protect her. They both went their different ways as they both left college but stayed in touch. Candace was a dancer and she was traveling the world between cruise lines and backup dancer for Dolly Parton and others while Blake was saving the world by working the Oil Spill. Candace moved back to Ocean Springs as she thought she was ready to settle down. She got married and finished her college degree and became an elementary school teacher. The year before Blake died; he spent his last Christmas with Candace. Candace had suffered from a terrible divorce and Blake knew some how she needed him.

Candace and Blake

They were both having a great time at my parent's home when they decided they wanted to take their party somewhere else. Sheree, Kathie's oldest daughter, volunteered to drive them both as they had already had enough to drink. Now everyone was there including Sheree's son Daryl (Lil D) and his girlfriend who both were about 15 years of age, and not to mention, the granddaughter of the Mayor of Biloxi. Now imagine, Lil' D is trying to impress this little girl and Blake loved any opportunity to stir up the family. As they were walking out the door, Blake hollered back at Lil' D, "You haven't plucked her flower yet?" Sheree slapped Blake on the back as they scooted out the door. Lil' D was so red and embarrassed, I never saw him bring her back to another family function again.

Blake and Candace hit a local bar downtown Ocean Springs and talked throughout the night. As the bar was ready to close, they called Aunt Happy (Kathie) to pick them up as they both had too much to drink to be driving. When she pulled up outside, everyone in the bar hollered at Blake, "Your Mom's here!"

All the way home, Blake kept saying, "Our Mom had to come pick us up from the bar!" and then he would let out that loud laugh that was like no other laugh. Then he kept telling Aunt Happy how much he loved her and Candace. Then all of a sudden, Aunt Happy noticed that it got awful quite. She figured they both passed out when all of a sudden from the back seat, Blake yelled "I call shotgun on the bed!" Candace hollered back at him, "The hell you say! That's my bed. You can sleep on the floor." When Aunt Happy pulled up in the drive way they both took off running. Blake starts stripping his clothes down to nothing when he jumped in Candace's bed stark naked. Candace hollered, "MOM, Blake's in my bed naked!" Candace had to sleep on the sofa because Blake was already passed out in her bed, naked!

When Blake died, I can remember Candace walking through the door and her face pale with disbelief. As the months went by,

Candace spent a lot of time with me as well as all of Blake's friends. She soon realized how much she meant to Blake through his friends that she barely knew.

Like all of us, Candace had to try to go on living without her best friend. She struggled as to her purpose in life and how to fill that void. Then Blake came to her in a dream-

"Candace's Dream"

Candace was on a plane flying to somewhere when she said that she felt a tap on her shoulder. She turned around and there he was, Blake sitting in the seat behind her. In disbelief, she said, "Blake, what are you doing here?" He just smiled at her with that big beautiful smile and said, "I have always wanted to travel with you, so here I am. I want to see the world with you, so where are we going next?"

Candace said when she woke-up; she knew at that moment she needed to change her life. She was not sure what was coming next when all of a sudden she ran into an old friend who is a Captain for a cruise ship. He asked her to join him on vacation and she went. When she got back, she quit her teaching job and took off with him to travel the Mediterranean and Europe. Within a few months, she was asked to consider coming back to dancing on the cruise ships. She took the job and she is back traveling the world, but this time, it is different. Blake is with her, right by her side, enjoying the world with her.

Candace and Blake (in spirit)

"If I ascend to heaven, thou are there! If I take the wings of the morning and dwell in the uttermost parts of the sea, even there thy hand shall lead me, and thy right hand shall hold me."
Psalms 139:8, 9-10

~Angelle~
(Flo)

Joose, Angelle (Flo) and Blake

Angelle Baudoin and Whitney are the same age and I met her when the two of them were cheering at high school. Angelle is a free spirited, fun loving, just a plain out happy person! It is no wonder why she is the way she is as both her parents, Ray and Mary Baudoin

305

are both the same way. When she started dating Joose, she became one of the guys as far as Blake was concerned. When I asked Angelle how she got the nickname "Flo", she told me that one day they were all sitting around trying to guess the meaning of Cajun words. Someone asked, "What was the meaning of floaton?" Angelle said, "I know! It is a floating piece of land mass." They all laughed as that was not what they thought it meant (dirty minds). Blake told her, "That's what I am going to call you. FLO!" He gave her that nickname and she has been called Flo ever since.

Blake loved Angelle with all his heart and she loved him too. They were like brother and sister. I think Blake just loved her personality. Like Blake, she was always trying to lift someone's spirits and between the two of them, people were drawn to their energy.

Blake and Flo at Lockport Parade

When we planned Blake's services, Angelle and her parents stepped in to help. Ray and Mary offered their camp down in Grand Isle so that we could all meet to celebrate his life. Mary shared with me the night that they got the call about the accident. She told me that her heart hurt so bad that she fell to her knees. Both Mary and Ray were on their back deck when she said all of a sudden there was a glow in the water shining so clear that they looked at each other in amazement. They had never seen something so beautiful as long as they had stayed at the camp so they knew it could only be a sign from Blake.

Mary and Blake

~Lauren~

Blake and Lauren

Lauren was Blake's high school sweetheart. The two of them were always together. I remember him telling me that Lauren's father said that he wished they had met later in life as he felt they were so young that he feared that they would separate once they got into college. Well, he was right. However they stayed very close through the years after high school. I can remember Blake telling me that he saw Lauren at a LSU game or at a party. He would always say, "Mah, she is still as pretty as ever."

I had not spoken to Lauren since they separated back in school, when the phone rang the next evening after Blake went down. Someone said, "Ms. Cindie, its Lauren." I grabbed the phone and started crying, "Oh Lauren, he is still missing." "I know, Ms. Cindie, but don't worry. I am talking with the Coast Guard and we are going

309

to find him!" She said calmly. "They found a tank that maybe his. I am calling everyone I know and we will not give up! Blake is a fighter and he is probably floating by the rig. Don't worry, I am on the phone with the Coast Guard and I will call you as soon as I hear anything." She said with hope in her voice. "Okay." I said with tears pouring down my face. "I love you." "I love you too." She said as she hung up the phone.

We both had so much hope, but the tank was not his and the Coast Guard had called off their search by that evening. Here is Lauren's story:

"The Friendship"
By Lauren Slowik

Jesse (Joose) Lagarde introduced Blake to me when I was in ninth grade, Blake in tenth. We started dating not long after that. We continued a relationship throughout our high school years growing up and experiencing life together until I went to college and we decided that we would remain great friends. Blake was whom I would call when I had any issue. He listened to me vent about my problems, made me smile when I was down, and always made me see the bright side of any situation life threw at me. He always laughed at me when I would talk about any other relationship I had and make me realize that I was probably being ridiculous and that the situation at hand was not as big of a deal as I was making it out to be. I think he thought I was a bit dramatic, which I am not at all! (haha). He remained very close to my dad and would always stop to visit him knowing he was lonely after my parent's divorce. Blake was always an extremely loyal friend and had a happiness about him that radiated to those around to him. He never took life to serious and lived every moment to the fullest. I always admired these traits about him and I to this day try to exert these qualities in my daily life.

From the day Blake went missing he visited me in my dreams. If he did not play a main role in the dream he was always a bystander, in a crowd, watching in the distance, I always knew he was there and even if the dream was unsettling or scary I felt safe knowing someone was looking after me. I knew I was not alone, he was there if I needed help. After a few months and many dreams I had **the dream** that would be the conclusion to these visits.

Experts have explained dreams as manifestations of our deepest desires and anxieties. I believe that we dream about things that are on our mind; our worries, upcoming events, our feelings, etc. In the spring of 2012, I was starting a new relationship with someone who was also very close to Blake. I had seen Drew at Blake's memorial but did not know how they knew each other. Come to find out his family's camp in Fourchon is next door to Johnny's camp, where Blake would spend most of his time. Blake spent many (I'm sure very entertaining) nights staying up talking with Drew and Drew's dad. He became very close to the family as he did with most people he encountered. Around the same time Drew and I were hitting it off, I was going to be a bridesmaid in my best friend Jackie's wedding.

As some may know when you serve in a wedding the wedding party has to get there earlier than the guests, stay after to take pictures, and meet everyone else at the reception following. Drew was going to the wedding with some of my friends and I was going to be meeting him at the reception. I believe that having these upcoming events on my mind is the reason for **the dream.**

"The Dream"
By Lauren Slowik

I remember that I was very dressed up and extremely excited. We just concluded Jackie's wedding ceremony and I was arriving at the reception with butterflies in my stomach. Seeing many people I know, walking from room to room, my main goal was to find Drew. It seemed like I was looking forever not having any luck. I was asking friends if they had seen him skimming each area hoping to lay my eyes on him. Finally I decided to walk upstairs to continue the search. As I am walking, scanning the upstairs area I made eye contact with one familiar person, he was in a wheelchair. I quickly did a double-take and realized it was Blake, only this time he was on crutches. As I blinked in confusion and intensely stared this time he was standing on his own smiling at me. I rushed towards him shouting, "Blake! What are you doing here?!" and as I reached out my arms to hug him, he turned away and there was Drew. He walked right through Blake to fill my outreached arms with a hug. I was so confused yet so happy I had finally found who I was looking for.

This was the last time Blake visited me in a dream. I am sure there are many different meanings to this dream but I think that this is Blake's way of saying that he trusts Drew. That he doesn't need to look after me anymore. For years Blake was a best friend and like a brother to me. I always knew I could call him for anything and he would always pick up the phone to listen or help in any way he could. I believe that Blake sent Drew to me to watch after me and make sure I am always safe, as he had done for so many years.

Drew and Lauren

~Meryl Marx~
Lauren's Mother -

Blake came into our lives when my daughter, Lauren, was 15. He was Lauren's first real boyfriend. He quickly became part of our family. Through the years Lauren and Blake remained very good friends. Time and distance never changed our family's relationship with him. I will forever love Blake. The following story happened while Blake and Lauren were dating:

313

"Angel in the Night"
By Meryl Marx

It was one of the most distressing darkest days in my professional life. I was returning from a business meeting; my flight landed in New Orleans at 11:30pm. The night was as dark as my mood. I was driving through dense fog with minimal visibility as I drove into the Raceland Lockport area. Suddenly I felt a jolt and heard a very loud scrapping noise coming from beneath the car. Simultaneously, the airbags blew out. I pulled off on the side of the deserted highway feeling such despair. I never felt more alone, scared and numb. I knew I needed to call someone but wasn't thinking clearly through the fog of my mind. I saw car lights pull up behind me and felt afraid knowing how alone I was on this lonely stretch of road at midnight. When I looked out the driver's side window I saw an angel. It was Blake. Fog surrounded him and he had a glow about him. In the eerie silence of the night, he said, "Ms Meryl, is that you? Are you ok?" I told him, "I am now as I cried through my tears....you are my angel."

~Reesa~

Blake and Reesa

Reesa and Blake started dating in college. I can remember the first time he told me about her, he was crazy about her. He said, "Mah, I am in love with a filly down the bayou." "She is awful young, Mah." He grinned. Then he showed me her picture on the computer and I was stunned. She was this beautiful slim French girl with deep brown eyes and dark black hair. I was shocked as most of the girls Blake had ever dated were usually a beautiful blond, not a brunette. She was stunning. They loved each other, but they were like two bulls in a china cabinet. Both strong headed and stubborn. When they split up, it was hard on all of us as Reesa had been with us for over four years. She was family and it was hard to say goodbye but Blake and her knew that if they stayed together, they would lose their friendship. They were friends first and they cared about each other's happiness.

The night Blake went missing, Reesa called me. She was in shock, "Ms. Cindie, is it true?" "Yes." I said. "Oh Ms Cindie, I can't believe it." She cried. "I know. I feel so helpless. I don't know what to do." I cried. The tears just kept flowing as we both just sat on the phone crying. Reesa came over the next morning to see me. I can remember the lost look in her eyes as it was still so unreal to both of us. We just sat together crying. Here is Reesa's dream that she wanted to share:

"My First Dream of Blake"
By Reesa Gravois

I was underneath Paige, Lance, & Ross Armstrong's carport at their mom & dad's house. There were many cars & trucks parked in the driveway. I was standing in between Paige's mother & father's cars, when out of nowhere Blake starts walking towards me. He had a glowing factor that was so beautiful radiating all around him. As astonished as I was to see him, knowing that he had died, I immediately started crying and yelled out, "Blake!!" He walked straight to me and hugged me for the longest. As I cried and cried, he continued to hold me. I backed up and said, "I thought you were dead! Your Mom is going to kill you! She just got a tattoo on her back for you!" He smiled at me with the most beautiful smile, and then I woke up.

The Night
By: Reesa Gravois

I remember when I heard the news that Blake had went down for a dive and never surfaced. I was at Cajun Palms, in Cabin Number 19, it was about 9:00 PM. We had taken a little family weekend getaway. As I was told what had happened, though there weren't many details, I remember being astonished. It just didn't make sense. Blake was the safest diver. All his friends and diving buddies knew it. Alicia Arabie, a close friend, rushed in our cabin and said that she needed to talk to me. Her face was pale and she looked terrified. As she uttered the words, "Blake never came up" I sat back and said to myself this isn't real. There is no possible way that he didn't resurface. "I know he is sitting on a rig right now, they just haven't found what rig." I just sat there in silence. After a while, I grabbed my phone and called everyone that I knew to find out what was going on; any tiny detail that I could get. Adrienne Besson was the first person I called. I knew Adam Cheramie would know. He and Blake were best friends. She told me that Adam was on the boat with him and that she didn't know much more than what I knew. After not hearing anything for a while, I decided I would call Mrs. Cindie. I figured she was a nervous wreck. She answered the phone and I said, "Mrs. Cindie, its Reesa." She immediately started sobbing. She said, "Reesa they can't find him. They can't find him. He never came up." I attempted to comfort her, "Mrs. Cindie, they will find him. I am telling you, he is ok. I'm sure he is fine. Don't worry about it. Take a deep breath." She cried and cried. I felt so helpless. I couldn't imagine the fear and anxiety that she was experiencing. Reality was, no words that came out of my mouth would make her feel better.

That night I couldn't sleep. I woke up every hour on the hour. Just imagining what they were doing on the water to find Blake. I just couldn't get him off of my mind. I couldn't imagine what had happened to him. Was he really dead? Rachel crossed my mind. The helplessness she must have felt when she found out the news. When Blake and I dated, my worst fear was for him to die on a dive. Sometimes when they got back to Fourchon from offshore, he

317

wouldn't call me. The things that would run through my head would make me feel so anxious. I would immediately jump to conclusions. Turned out that he just had a buzz and forgot to call me! I soon realized that this was real life for Rachel. The fear that I once felt, she was feeling but not only for herself, for their son as well.

Guardian Angel
By: Reesa Gravois

Blake is one of the most amazing people that I have known. The way he lived his life day in and day out, without regret, can only motivate others to live the same way. That kind of motivation comes few and far between. Family was very important to Blake.

He was the rock of his family, as Mrs. Cindie would agree. Every time something would go wrong he was the first to call. His passion, over anything else in this world was the water. He loved diving. I think if he had to choose, diving over women; he would choose diving without a doubt. That's saying a lot, knowing how much he loved women. Whether it was to spearfish or to cut rope out of a wheel of a boat, he would be excited to do it. He always said that when you are underwater, everything around you moves so much faster. You're so vulnerable; it's a whole different world. He practically lived in Fourchon during the summer. He called Fourchon his paradise. "What more do you need?" he would say.

He made a community of Fourchon. He knew everyone there and every weekend was a party full of laughter, music, and good times. His "dancing shoes" were always ready. Boy did he think he could dance. It was more like a crouched bounce he would do with his hands in the air. Many laughs and many life experiences I cherished with him. I am truly honored to have been a part of Blake's life. Although God took him early, he lived a full life. No day was ever wasted. He is sitting in heaven gazing down at all of us, watching over us. He is forever our guardian angel.

*"We cannot pass our guardian
angel's bounds, resigned or sullen,
he will hear our sighs."
Saint Augustine*

~Rachel~

Rachel and Blake

Rachel came into Blake's life un-expectantly. Blake was finally getting settled with his business and he knew what he wanted in life and then WHAM! Here she was this beautiful blond knock-out who had just graduated out of LSU College. She was a huge LSU fan and her life was Baton Rouge. Nobile had introduced them and they both hit it off right away. They became inseparable and spent a lot of time together. Of course summer time in Grand Isle and winter time, football season in Baton Rouge. It was the first time I saw Blake settling down. He was the happiest in his life and I knew that they loved each other instantly. I felt like this was it and he is going to settle down now. When Rachel found out she was pregnant, I was ecstatic. Blake was a family man and I knew his values of raising a family with both parents were very important to him. They were so happy.

Blake and Rachel

That night when I called Rachel that was the hardest thing I had ever had to do. She was numb and I was numb. How were we going to get through this, I can remember thinking to myself? How will she raise this child without his Father? Those questions were running through my mind, but nothing prepared me for what we had to plan next…HIS FUNERAL SERVICES! Here this beautiful girl carrying my son's child was going to have to do the hardest thing anyone could imagine and that is help plan a funeral of the man she loved. She should have been planning a wedding, not a funeral. Here the man she loved, the man who told her to not worry as he gleamed with excitement of becoming a father; the man who vowed that he would take care of her for the rest of her life was now gone. How were we ever going to get through this?

Rachel and baby Hank

Even Pirates Go to Heaven

~Tina's White Rose~

The most recent message from Blake was at Mike Toups' sister, Tina's funeral services. Mike, Ponce's dad dearly loved Blake as his own son as the boys were always together and they stayed many a nights at his home. Tina was born mentally handicapped and she never was able to be independent. Since the age of nine, she lived in a nursing home and spent every weekend and holiday with family and friends. When their parents died, Big Brother, Mike took care of her. Like Mike, Tina was no stranger to Ponce's friends. The one friend she loved so much was Blake. Her heart would melt every time she saw him. Of course, he loved every minute of it. September 13, 2013, Tina passed away from cancer.

My heart was saddened as I know how much Tina meant to Mike and had Blake been here, he would have dropped everything to be there to support Mike during this time. The night before her services, I could not sleep. I had not planned to go to her services as I had a service man coming by the house and I had to be home to let him in the house. All night I kept hearing Blake's voice telling me, "Mah, I need you to go to Tina's service." "Mah, please!!!" is all I kept hearing in my head until finally I changed my clothes; told the service guy to lock the house when he leaves and rushed to Lockport as I was pushing close to her services starting.

As I was turning down LA 1, I heard Blake tell me, "Mah, stop and pick up a white rose to bring." I said out loud, "BLAKE, NO WAY will I make it in time!" "Mah, pick up a white rose...you will make it." I heard his voice in my head. Reluctantly, I stopped at the grocery store in Matthews for a rose. There was one white rose in the store. As I pulled in the Church, I felt this warm feeling that Blake was with me and that he was so glad that I was there. I could hear his voice, "Thank you, Mom." I felt as though it was not me walking in that Church, but Blake as I continued down the aisle.

There stood Mike with tears as he looked at me walking in. His first words were, "I hoped you would come." We embraced and shared our warm memories of both Tina and Blake. I handed him the white rose and said to him, "Mike, for some reason Blake wanted me to give this rose to you. I assumed he wanted to give it to Tina." Mike took the rose and placed it in Tina's hands before they closed her casket. As I left the services, I was so grateful that Blake sent me as I knew the minute I walked in the door that I was sent for a reason. I knew that I had to be there.

On November 19th, my sister Kathie sent me an email message. Kathie had no clue who Mike was or about his sister, Tina. Little did I know at that time, the importance of the white rose Blake had me give to Mike until now?

A dear friend called me one morning to tell me about the dream he had of his father, who had passed on suddenly a few months before. He told me that in his dream, his father met him, and they walked and talked amid beautiful fields under a warm, sunny sky. As they walked, they passed an unusual field of white roses. What my friend found unusual about the field was that each white rose stood alone on a single stem, and each had a ribbon around it. They covered the field by the thousands and looked to be untouched by human hands, yet they grew perfectly. In his dream, my friend asked his father about the unusual field of roses, and why each had a ribbon around it. His father explained to him that each rose was a gift, sent to the earth that was never received. So the roses stand, each with its ribbon, to be given to the soul upon their return to the hereafter. My friend didn't understand, so he pressed his father further, and the story he was told is one that I have heard many times from the souls who communicate to their families on the earth. Each of us, in our lifetime on the earth, is sent many gifts from the hereafter. Some are the gift of laughter when things are bleak, others are the gift of friendship for the lonely. Some are even true love for those who walk the earth in search of it. These gifts are sent to us to help encourage us on our journey, and to take the sometimes rough edges off a difficult time we experience, or a heartache we endure. So what are they doing, standing in rows like soldiers, in the hereafter? They were gifts unopened by us--ignored for some reason, passed by, uncollected, and returned to the hereafter so that we have them when we understand their value. My friend's dream is not unusual--the souls have told me many times that we are showered with things from the hereafter to make our lives a little easier, but because of fear, distrust, or sometimes plain stubbornness, we are unable to see these gifts for what they truly are. Worse--we acknowledge they are gifts, but somehow feel we are not entitled to them or unworthy. Many of us are in stages of our lives where we do not trust people or circumstances enough to take a chance, fearing we will be worse off than when we started. The souls have a very simple message to the earth which they have stated over and over--gifts come to us because they are meant to. There is no need to question why or how--gifts are not planned, but they correspond to circumstances in our lives the same way friends remember a birthday with a gift. People who wander into our lives when we need a friend is a special gift, although many are turned away out of fear or distrust. Opportunities for good things to happen come and go because we think too much about them. But nothing given to us is ever lost--even though it was sorely needed by us on the earth and we still did not accept it, these gifts return to the hereafter, and wait for us to cross over and understand why they were sent in the first place. It is the very point, however, that we no longer need them. So they return to the hereafter, objects of kindness and love, and grow like beautiful roses in a field of white. I have said many times throughout the years that bereavement is a bonfire of the vanities--it is a point where we hit the bottom of our emotional, physical and philosophical barrel. This is exactly the time that we need to look around us and grab hold of whatever can keep us from disappearing into the black hole of grief. If you are bereaved, or alone, or unhappy in a place on your journey, then look around you-- the gifts may not be obvious but they are there. Don't just accept them, grab them with both hands and hang on to them--they were meant to save your hope and help your soul. And they are meant for you. Accept whatever comes your way with the knowledge that somebody, whether it is here or hereafter, is concerned for you and values you. All you are required to do is say "thank you."

By Medium George Anderson, www.georgeanderson.com

Blake and Tina Toups

The white rose was not for Tina but was a gift from Tina to Mike. Blake and Tina sent us both a message to say that they loved us. The white rose was a gift from the hereafter. I can just envision Tina walking through those fields of roses telling Blake she wants to send a rose to Mike. How else could he help her but through me? I was the messenger. The white rose was a symbol of both Tina and Blake's love and comfort for Mike and that I might have missed if I had not been paying attention.

In my heart, Blake is not gone for good but that he is still here among each of us. He loved each and every one of us and as he promised me, he was going to find a way to reach us no matter what. If we are not paying attention, you can bet that we have beds of white roses waiting for us when we enter the gates of heaven because Blake has

327

been working very hard to reach us with signs and gifts from the hereafter.

"Thank You, Baby! I love you!" Mom.

Blake and Me at Whitney and Daniels Wedding

Chapter 51

A Son of a Sailor

By Cindie Roussel

The day Hank was born it should have been the happiest day of our life but it was an emotional day for me as I could not help but think that Blake should have been there. On December 29th, the Oschner's Hospital halls were filled with people anxiously awaiting Blake Anthony Terry, Jr. (aka Hank's) arrival. We had lap-tops and cell phones relaying messages back to the world of minute-by-minute updates of Rachel and Hank's condition. You would have thought you were at an LSU game with over 40 people tail-gating in the hospital parking lot. As each report came in, you could hear a pin drop in the waiting room until the final message came over the line...HE'S HERE!!!!!

Our hearts were filled with joy as we all waited for this day to finally come. Hank arrived weighing 6 lbs 7 oz. 19 inches with big blue-eyes and a head full of sun-kissed hair as though he had been at Fourchon all week with his Daddy catching Tuna! What a bittersweet moment. Between tears of joy and tears of sadness all at once was overwhelming. Hank was finally here!

I can remember the day Blake told me that Rachel was pregnant. He seemed to be in disbelief as he was telling me over the phone. He said, "Mah, one of the soldiers got past the gate." I knew right away what he meant. I can remember feeling excited as Blake had done everything he could possibly have done in one man's lifetime, and having a child would be his greatest achievement in his life.

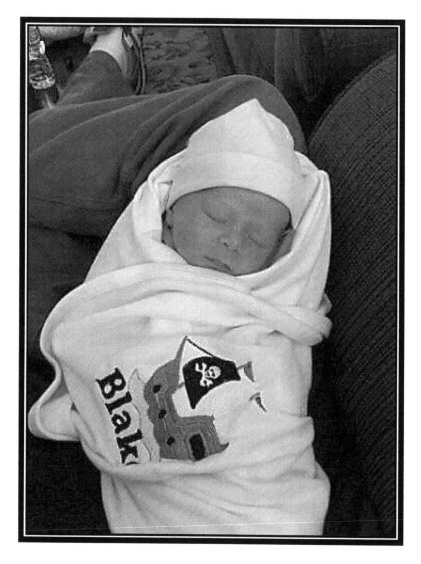

Blake Anthony Terry, Jr. (Hank)

A Son of a Sailor

He loved children and he would be an excellent father. He had all the family values and this was a new chapter in his life.

Rachel told Blake not to tell anyone until they told her parents, however, Blake told everyone. He was so excited. He told me right away; he told his Grandma; he told his friends; he told the lady at the grocery check-out line; he told everyone! He was so excited about being a father that he wanted the world to know.

Before he left on his fishing trip, we were planning to have a party at Rachel's parents to celebrate the gender of the baby. Blake and Rachel were planning to meet with the doctor on Tuesday and then make the announcement if they were having a boy or girl. Rachel was ordering a cake so that when you cut open the cake it would be pink on the inside for a girl or blue for a boy. I was making baby bibs to give to Rachel for a gift. I had them all laid out on the bed when Blake came in through the back door. I asked him what he thought about the bibs and he said that Rachel was going to love them and then he paused for a moment. I can remember he had this funny look on his face as though he knew for some reason something was going to happen. He said, "Mah, we find out next week, ya know?" "Yes, baby, I know." I replied. I can remember that he seemed as though something strange was going to happen. He just looked down, holding one of the bibs in his hands. At that moment I thought, "he must be scared." I told him, "Blake, it is going to be okay." He looked up at me and said, "I know" and then he looked at me with a grin and he said, "It's a boy, you know." I said, "Yes, I am sure of it."

But now, I wonder if he had a clue that something was going to happen? That maybe telling me that they were going to find out about the baby would convince him that everything was going to be okay. By saying it would mean that it was going to happen. He knew

I was making those bibs for their party, so why would he tell me what I already knew? Did God give him a sign somehow?

The next several months were a roller coaster. I was so worried about Rachel and the baby that I had to make them my focus. All I kept thinking was I had to take care of her as Blake would want me to do this. He is not here and she needs us. During all this time, Whitney and Daniel found out they were having their first child, Cameron. The night she tried to tell me, I was in disbelief as I was still in shock over Blake, worried about Rachel and the baby and now Whitney? I look back now as I was not there for Whitney. When she needed her mother the most, here she was becoming a mother. I was in so much shock with losing Blake that I could not balance both girls being pregnant at the same time. Whitney held it together for me and I can never pay her back for all she did. I was really out of it and everything started to unfold on me. The afternoon that Rachel went into labor, I fell to my knees in front of the nurse's station crying because Blake should have been there. I could remember Kathie grabbing me up and telling me that he was there. That he was with her and that everything was going to be okay. I was so torn-up inside because he was not going to be there to see his son born and have that wonderful moment of holding his child in his arms. How unfair all of this was as he was a good man and he did not deserve to not be able to have that wonderful blessing. How unfair it was for Rachel to not have him there by her side to hold her hand and comfort her. How unfair it was that Whitney could not have her mother there because I was in pieces. How so unfair it all was and at that moment I fell to my knees and I cursed God screaming, "WHY? OH GOD, WHY? HOW COULD HE NOT BE HERE? WHY GOD WHY?"

When Hank arrived, everyone shouted in the waiting room with excitement, "HE'S HERE! HE'S HERE!" Scott and I embraced each other and we could not stop crying. I don't remember who was there I just remember holding Scott and crying. We were overwhelmed with emotion as Hank was finally here. He was safe, healthy and he was FINALLY HERE!

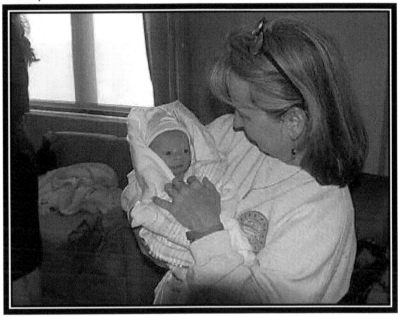

Me and Hank

"*May those who sow in tears reap with shouts of joy! He that goes forth weeping bearing the seed for sowing shall come home with shouts of joy, bringing his sheaves with him.*" *Psalms 126: 5-6*

Chapter 52

The Whole World Calls Me "Hank"

By Cindie Roussel

The next couple of months, we had no idea what we were up against. Blake and Rachel had not been married and he was lost in the Gulf so we had no death certificate. We had no DNA and no marriage licenses to prove that Blake Jr. was his son. Here we have his child, his beautiful child that by the state of Louisiana, we had no way to name him after his father, Blake Anthony Terry. Blake Jr. left the hospital with no name on his birth certificate. All we had were emails and text messages to prove Blake knew of his child being born. Blake did not even know Blake Jr. was going to be a boy. He had nick named the baby Hank, whether girl or boy. He felt like the baby was a boy all along, but had not been told yet. See his message to Rachel while she was pregnant with Hank:

On Tue, Jun 21, 2011 at 12:39 PM,
*Blake Terry <**yrretllub@yahoo.com**> wrote:*
Hank is a he and he needs some solid meat for lunch such as a steak or a whole chicken maybe. He also needs some fruit juice preferably apple but anything other than v8 will work just fine. Hank loves all sides and he def needs a well-balanced desert. Make sure his ice cream has sprinkles, nuts, sundae fudge and whipped cream. If his meal order is met today u will have a good morning Tom! Sent from my iPhone

Rachel and Blake had planned to visit the doctor the Tuesday after he had died. We were planning to all meet at Rachel's parents so that they could announce the sex of the baby that day. Blake was shooting grouper on Saturday to fry at her parents on Tuesday and then the accident happened. Our whole world fell apart. None of us had imagined something so horrific would happen. Now we had to prove this baby was his baby.

I contacted DNA services of America to find out if Tony, Blake's father and I could be tested to prove we were Blake Jr.'s grandparents. What I learned was something so remarkable. The representative explained that both of us could be tested but the results would only prove 80/90% that the baby was part of our blood line. However, if Blake had a male sibling, the bloodline was 99/100% accurate. I called Dustin right away. Shaken with tears and emotion, Dustin said, "Mom, what a gift I could give back to my brother."

Jr., Dustin, Tony and Hank (Nobile is in the background)

The next day Rachel and Jr. headed to DNA of America in Baton Rouge and Dustin headed to the DNA of America in Houma. When Rachel arrived, the nurse asked her for Hank's information and then turned to Jr. and asked him for his driver's license. Both of them looked at each other and then realized that the nurse must have thought that Jr. was the Father. Both laughed and said, "No, he is not the Father. The Father's brother is being tested in Houma." Then they both laughed again and realized what they had said.

The next few days moved quickly. It took about 2 weeks for the results to come in. I was in Miami working when I got the call from our representative. She said, "Ms. Cindie, I have the results. Blake Jr. is 100% match to the Terry bloodline."

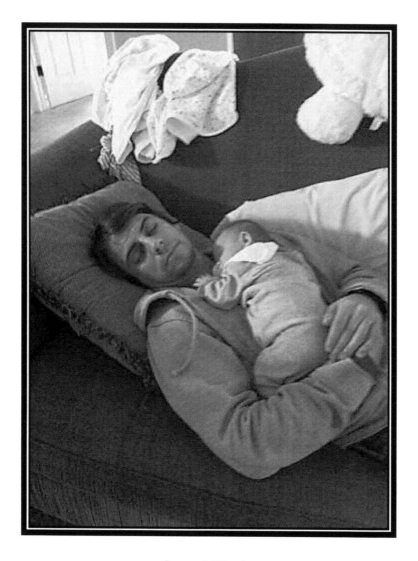

Jr. and Hank

Tears poured down my face as I knew he was in my heart, but to hear someone tell me this was just overwhelming. We had something to bring before the judge, we had proof.

Case 8046536	Sample One	Sample Two
Name	Blake A. Terry	Dustin Terry
Race	Caucasian	Caucasian
Date Collected	1/30/2012	1/31/2012
Test No.	8046536-Y1	8046536-Y2
Locus	Allele Sizes	Allele Sizes
DYS456	15	15
DYS389 I	13	13
DYS390	24	24
DYS389 II	29	29
DYS458	17	17
DYS19	14	14
DYS385 a/b	10 13	10 13
DYS393	13	13
DYS391	10	10
DYS439	13	13
DYS635	23	23
DYS392	13	13
Y GATA H4	12	12
DYS437	14	14
DYS438	12	12
DYS448	18	18

DNA Test Report

DDC is accredited/certified by AABB, CAP, ACLASS-International, ISO/IEC 17025, CLIA, NYSDOH & ASCLD/LAB-International.

Interpretation:

Y-Chromosome STR testing was done to determine relatedness of the tested individuals. According to the information obtained from the testing, the results are consistent with individuals that share a common male lineage.

Subscribed and sworn before me on February 9, 2012

Edward Harris
Notary Public, State of Ohio
My Commission Expires October 10, 2013

I, the undersigned Laboratory Director, verify that the interpretation of the results is correct as reported on 2/9/2012.

Michael L. Baird, Ph.D.
Marco Scarpetta, Ph.D.
Tricia D. Frye, Ph.D.

Thomas M. Reid, Ph.D.
Richard Chmelo, Ph.D.

DNA Results

The next month we sat in a court room ready to provide whatever we could to give Blake Jr. his name. I can remember how nervous I was as we had been to court two times previously over Blake's succession and tried to name Hank, Blake Jr. and the Judge was not compassionate but rather cold. He made each person go through the details of what happened the night that Blake made his last dive. It was as though he wanted to hear the story over and over while it destroyed each person who had to relive that night. But then came the Judgment to declare Blake Jr. to be named after his father.

My stomach was in knots as we sat again in another court room expecting the worse with this Judge and got what we expected. He told us that he could not help us but that we had to bring this case to another jurisdiction where Blake Jr. was born, Baton Rouge Court House. So we had to wait for several more months for another court date. Blake Jr. had no name on his birth certificate. He could not get insurance because he had no social security number because of no name on birth certificate. What a mess! Finally we got a court date. Rachel, Kathi Walker, Rachel's mother and I show up in Baton Rouge Court House.

If you have never been in a civil court room, then you are in for an experience. People are everywhere fighting charges such as drugs, delinquent on child support, not paying tickets or abusing each other. Just about anything. The worst part is that you have to sit and listen to every case. Each case is worse than the one before. The Judge is different in every court room. Some have patience to listen while others are tired of the same crap and they sentence the crime for 30 days and pay the clerk.

We waited patiently in our section going over what we thought the Judge may ask us when in walks Judge LWW. I knew then, only Blake could have picked this Judge to name his son. She looked like Halli Berry with long brown hair and beautiful tan skin. She had four people sitting in front of her each with laptops running that would respond to what she needed instantly. Searching sites and printing documents right there. She meant business. I looked up to the heavens and winked. I knew she was our Judge.

First Rachel got on the stand and she had to tell how both she and Blake met. She went through all the events that led up to that night of the accident. I can remember her face and mouth shaking, but she held it together. All I could remember was thinking, "I cannot do this. Oh dear God, I cannot do this." Then she asked me to approach the stand. She asked me if Blake knew about Hank. She asked a few more questions but I really don't remember. All I remember was telling her how excited he was about Hank and that we were all happy. Then Kathi Walker got on the stand and I fell apart. The court room had become so silent that I think every bench filled up in the court room as she began to tell her story.

She told how Blake was the one that insisted Rachel tell her parents that she was pregnant. How he was the one who walked outside to speak to Rachel's father, Gary Walker. How he was the one that felt that it was his obligation to tell her parents and to reassure them that she and the baby would never have to worry as he would take care of both of them for the rest of their lives. How he loved her and that he respected them both and that family was so important to him.

The whole time, the judge kept looking at me with this smile that it was as though I could read her mind. It was the look of how proud you must be to of had such a wonderful son. She was speaking directly to me through her eyes as though we were the only two people in that crowded court room. It was a look of how proud you must be that he was such a good man; a young man who was full of compassion and love that only a mother could want from a son. She kept smiling at me and I did all I could to hold back the tears, but I could not. I just wept the whole time as I was proud. I was so proud that he cared so much about the importance of a family and raising a child in a warm loving home. I was so proud but my heart just could not hold back the tears because he was not here to follow through. He was not going to be here to do what he promised.

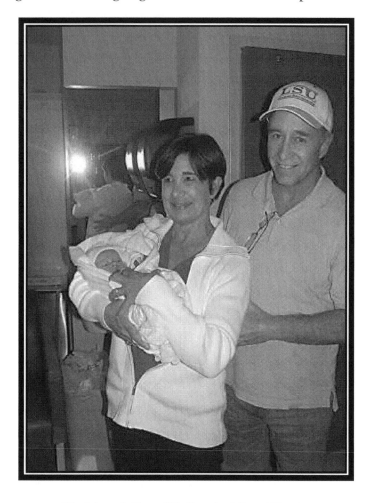

Kathi and Gary Walker holding Hank

Finally, the judge read her decision. The words were the most heartwarming words I have ever heard.

"It is ordered, adjudged and decreed that Blake Anthony Terry, whose date of birth is March 21, 1984, is declared to be the father of the male child born to Rachel Claire Walker, a single woman, on the 29th day of December, 2011 at Ochsner Hospital in the City of Baton Rouge, Parish of East Baton Rouge, State of Louisiana. It is further ordered, adjudged and decreed that said minor child shall bear the surname of his biological determined father, namely Terry, and said child shall be known and his birth registered in the name of Blake Anthony Terry, Jr. It is further ordered, adjudged and decreed that the Department of Vital Records for the State of Louisiana is ordered to add the father's name, Blake Anthony Terry, to the birth certificate and change the baby's name, currently "Unnamed Walker", to Blake Anthony Terry, Jr. to reflect his father's name. Judgment read, rendered and signed this 14th day of March 2012 in Baton Rouge, Louisiana. – The Honorable LWW, Judge"

You could have heard a pin drop from that court room full of people who were fighting over child support, abuse of each other and not wanting to claim their children to get out of supporting them. The shame they must have felt. Here three women were standing together holding back the tears and pleading for a child to have his father's name. Who his father WANTED him to have his name but could not be here to fight for his rights. How small their problems must have been to them to hear Kathi tell them how good of a man my son was. I was proud and happy for the first time in months. I could not stop crying. I think at that point, I could never ever hear anything more beautiful than those words the Judge read in that court room that day. How she must have known what it meant to us for her to declare Blake Jr. to be the son of Blake. I hope that what she did that day was one of her greatest blessings she experienced as a Judge and that on days that are not so good, she can reflect back on that day of bringing our family this wonderful gift. Blake Jr. finally received his birth certificate after four months of his birth.

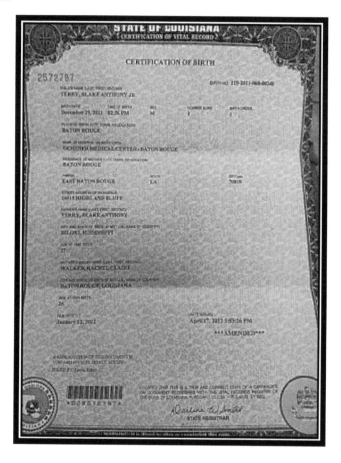

**Blake Anthony Terry Jr. son of Blake Anthony Terry
Birth Certificate (4 months after his birth)**

The next several months we started the next court battle for Blake, Jr. to receive his father's social security. Kathi and I continued to fight for Blake Jr. to have Blake's benefits. The problem we had was we were unable to receive a death certificate. We wrote several letters to Vital Records and then to our local congressman after hiring two different attorneys and still no luck. The issue we had was that Blake died 70 miles from the Louisiana Coast Line and that the State of Louisiana would not issue a death certificate because he did not die in Louisiana according to the Attorney Supervisor. Social Security would not issue Blake Jr. his Father's benefits without a death certificate. We were caught up in a vicious loop.

Kathi and I began to start researching and digging to find someone to listen to us. Finally, after several letters we wrote to our local Government Representatives, the Governor of the State of Louisiana and then to the President, Rachel received a call from the State. She was informed that she would be receiving a check to include back-pay from the date Blake Jr. was born. On March 21st, 2013, Blake Sr.'s birthday, Blake Jr. received his Father's benefits. Fifteen months after Blake Jr. was born. We all believed that this was Blake Sr.'s birthday wish for his son. Thank you, Blake!

THE WHITE HOUSE
WASHINGTON

March 19, 2013

Dear Blake Terry:

Thank you for writing to President Obama. The President appreciates your taking the time to share your views and concerns. We received your correspondence and forwarded your information to the appropriate agency for further review. You may also find assistance by visiting www.USA.gov or calling 1-800-FED-INFO.

Sincerely,

The Office of Presidential Correspondence

Chapter 53

Messages from Heaven

By Cindie Roussel

I woke up half-dressed wondering how I got here. I looked around the room as I did not recognize the place. Was I in a hotel room? I had no money, no keys and no clothes. I tried calling for someone to bring me clothes but I could not get anyone on the phone. I walked out of the room and people were everywhere. I was ashamed as I was partially dressed. All of a sudden, rolling smoke started coming towards us so we all ran into the stair well.

The stairs were full of people, some dressed, some partially dressed and some even naked. No one seemed to care as everyone was trying to climb the stairs. The stairs were strange as each level was not connected so some were hanging off the edges pulling themselves up by the rails. I was so scared then I felt this arm reach out. It was Blake. His face was glowing with that beautiful smile. He was wearing a deep blue t-shirt and he had this beautiful look about him. He said, "Mom, it's okay, I am on the third level now. I have prepared your home for you and I have everything you need." "Mah, it is beautiful here. It is more than you could ever imagine." "I love you, Mom." Then, I WOKE UP! I was stunned. What did he mean by the third level?

What did all this mean for me to be partially clothed? Since my dream of Blake calling me on my cell phone, several of family and friends have shared with me of dreams that they have had of Blake. Each dream, Blake shared where he was headed and what he was doing. In one particular instance, Blake reached out to two people that had no connection to each other but he shared where he had been and where he was headed next. One is a dream from Natalie, my niece and the other from Jr.

January 5ᵗʰ, 2012 –
Hi Aunt Cindie-

I hope your holidays were the best they could be. I can only imagine the difficulty. Blake Jr. is so gorgeous. I wish I could see his sweet face. I know he has been such a blessing.

The reason I am writing is a dream I had last night. I feel compelled to share. In the dream, I was on my way to work. Making my way through the crowded building, I see in the distance a man in a silver suit (literally a silver glitter suit). He was sitting at a coffee kiosk. Immediately, the man captured my attention. As I got closer, the man turned around. Much to my surprise, I knew this man in the wild suit. It was Blake. He wore no shirt under this suit and was incredibly tan. When he saw that I recognized him, he got the biggest smile on his face and started doing this silly dance with the suit that I can absolutely see him doing. Once I reached him, he gave me a very long hug. Then, he looked in my face and said, "Wow, Nat. You look so happy." Still stunned at his presence for so many reasons, I managed to mutter, "Blake? What are you doing here?" He told me he had just visited Candace. Now it was my turn. He said again, "You look so happy. I'm glad. I'll be seeing you. I'm goin' to Grandmah's Bible study." And that quick, he was gone. Short and to the point. I woke smiling through tears. I felt like this was such a gift and message in a way. He sees us all. He is very much still in the daily lives of those that he loved. I'm grateful, however estranged we were, that I had the opportunity to see his face again. Truly a gift. I hope this message doesn't offend you in any way. I just felt so strongly that this might be a message you needed/wanted to hear. Please pass along to Candace; I have no way to share this with her.

I love you ALL. God Bless you always. And congratulations on Blake, Jr. He's truly beautiful – Nat.

January 8ᵗʰ, 2012- 8:21am - Good morning. Hope you had a great time at the game and an all around great weekend!... I meant to email you sooner. Friday morning I had a dream about Blake. Can't remember all the details, but we were talking over the phone similar to the dream you had. We spoke briefly. He told me that he was visiting at Grandma's and was still trying to get his business started, which seems very appropriate beings he was there for the Friday night Terry cookout! But he still seems very motivated on completing his work. This is the first time I've dreamt about him and I woke up with a more comforting feeling, rather than being upset and short of breath... He didn't tell me where he was going next or when I'd hear from him again, but we def need to keep his phone on for future calls! Love you, Allen (Jr.)

Through each dream, Blake told me as he had promised, "I will let you know where I am headed next." Blake had visited each sharing his time with Candace and Natalie, his cousins and then going to bible study with Grandma. Not something I ever thought I would hear from Blake. In all dreams, he was smiling and dancing and letting each of us know how much he loved us. He was wearing clothes that shined and he had a glow about him. He had told each of us he was working. Working on what, who knows? Maybe God has a boat that he likes to take out fishing. Maybe Peter and Paul is his deck crew and Blake is teaching them where to find the best Tuna. Maybe Blake is helping God decide on the perfect sunset or a rainbow over the horizon. No matter what, Blake continues to be helping someone, as he did here on Earth, sharing that wonderful smile and laughter.

Blake has not only come to us in dreams, he has also been with us at celebrations. This next dream will show you just how close heaven and earth really are…

During his 1st year of missing Mardi Gras, Blake visited Dustin, his brother. He asked if Dustin had everything ready for Mardi Gras parade in Lockport. Mardi Gras was a big event to Blake as weeks prior to the event, planning of keg stands, arm wrestling tables and costumes were underway. I would make costumes, usually all night before the parade as Blake was always last minute in deciding what he wanted. Or the idea of what theme he wanted just did not come to him until last minute. However, this particular year, Blake was not here to do the planning. Dustin and Jr. made the plans having 12 costumes and cannon to shoot jello-shots from the back of the truck. They had a life size picture of Blake from the previous year with a costume specially made for him to drape over. In addition, they had me make Hank his own costume as the plan was to bring him for all to hold up as the prince of Mardi Gras. Their idea was somewhat like the lion king. Now understand, none of these people were walking or riding floats but only dressing up in costumes as they have always done in the past.

During Dustin's dream, he told Blake of the plans expecting Blake to be disappointed that they forgot something, but Blake was not. He reached out his arms to hug Dustin and he told him that he had it all together and that he was proud of him. He then told him that he had to leave as he had work to do but he would be back for the parade. Dustin told him that he was worried that this would be the last time he would see him, but Blake reassured him not to worry. He gave Dustin a big hug and Dustin woke up with tears running down his face.

The parade day came and it was a very cold and cloudy day. Rachel dropped off Hank to meet Dustin and the crew in Lockport. I told her that I thought it would be best not to bring Hank as it was cold and I was afraid he may get sick. She seemed okay, but I could tell she was a little disappointed. Later that morning, Dustin called me telling me that I needed to bring Hank. He insisted and I am so glad I did. Little did I know Blake would reveal such a special moment in a dream. Through a friend, Flo shared a dream of one of Blake's friends, Lori.

A few weeks after mardi gras Lori dreamt about Blake. She said he was making a quick trip to thib and HAD to stop in and say hey. He was SO excited to tell her that he was able to make it to the Lockport parade this year!!!!(chills) He continued to tell her how amazing it was to see little Hank for the first time and was so proud to be a daddy!! (more chills) Mrs Cindie I NEVER doubt he's still checking up on us... And isn't missing a thing that's going on! I was always amazed at everything on Earth BT was able to make it too! I can about imagine angel Blake! Haha He's everywhere at every party we have! I know it! Flo

The Bible tells us in 2nd Corinthians, 12:2, Paul's vision of a man in Christ who fourteen years ago was caught up to the third heaven. Whether it was in the body or out of the body I do not know, but God knows- he was caught up to Paradise. What does this mean? Is Blake telling me he is in the third heaven? Is Blake in Paradise? I trust the Lord that he is in paradise.

"Yes, Blake, the connection might not be good, but you are reaching me. I will keep the lines open until we see each other again. I love you, Mom."

Lockport Parade

Chapter 54

The Blake Terry Memorial Foundation (BTMF)

By Cindie Roussel and Derrick Rotolo

When we built the Blake Terry Memorial Foundation (BTMF), little did any of us know how large this organization would grow? We grossed over $110 thousand in revenue in the first two years. Our main goal was to draw awareness to families and friends on what to do and how to take action if something were to happen to their loved ones during a diving event. I wrote "Burning Daylight" right after Blake's accident as I was still in shock and I knew that I did not want anyone to go through what we did. This book provides some direction of what to do; who to call and brings awareness of the dangers involved with diving. The organization started out with over 30 members and continues to grow every year. As with any new organization, we have had our ups and downs trying to get started. What none of us ever thought about was how to put our rescue plan into place until one day, Father's day 2013, we got our first call. The diver had been fishing in the Gulf with friends when he went missing. The feelings and memories came like a flood of fear all over again. We had the funds…the boats…the people…but we were not prepared for those feelings to resurface. I can remember telling Nobile, "You have got to do this for me, Nobile. We need you." Nobile replied, "I cannot dive." "I know, just be there for the family." I replied. "I need for you to head this up for us." As the calls kept coming in, the hope was there that maybe, just maybe we would find him. As the hours turned to days, the hope diminished and we had to call off the search. I can remember one of the diver's family members asked, "What do I tell the family?" "Tell them that we did all we could and that there is nothing more that can be done." I replied. That was the hardest words I had ever had to say to anyone.

In the past 4 years, we had 4 divers die. Two were recovered and two were lost in the Gulf. I never dreamed I would be looking at recovery equipment such as side-scan sonar systems that can detect up to 600 meters below the surface; or trying to raise funds to build a Seaman's Memorial so that I can have a burial place for my son because I had nothing but his bag from the boat. No body, no mask, no gun…NOTHING. No trace of him…lost to the Gulf. I am merely a mother that wants to prevent this from happening to another mother. This is not the June Cleaver life I dreamed I would be living, but here I am.

Through the BTMF, we hope to bring awareness that will stop these accidents as well as help others who have gone through this horrible ordeal.

For more information, visit our website –
www.btmemorialfoundation.com.

The Blake Terry Memorial Foundation

Below is a story by Derrick Rotolo, my dear friends, Jacque and Debbie's son:

"The Light that came from the Dark"

The day in question was as normal as any other day, but when we were getting ready for bed, a phone call stopped us in our tracks. It was my aunt saying that my cousin Blake had been lost at sea. When we arrived at my aunt's house, we received the details about the accident, and everyone was waiting for news on what the divers had found. Everyone was in a state of shock, and we were waiting for a call. After waiting for some time, a call came in, and we finally got the full story. Blake had gone on a dive and never came back to the surface. Blake's friends had been searching for him, but there was no sign of Blake. The family was just waiting for any word. The wait was terrible, but there was still hope that he would be found. We all hoped that Blake had lost his sense of direction and was waiting for help. His friends said that they never saw him come to the surface; therefore, hope began to fade away. Every second felt like hours, and we knew that as each minute passed the chances of finding him were getting lower and lower. However, no one gave up on that tough country boy; we waited for the message that would never come. The search was called off after a few days, and the weeks that followed were filled with sadness and grief. The family had no answers, and the wake would be held without a body. The family was still reeling from the unexpected loss of a son, brother, father, and all around good guy. My aunt was a loving person, but she wasn't the same after this accident. She didn't have the joy that she possessed before the death of her son. The time passed so slowly that a month felt like years, and everyone felt saddened by the loss of such a kind person. Blake Terry was one wild character, but he would give you the shirt off of his back. This is why he was missed by his family and his friends. Blake was the life of the party and always had a smile on his face. He always had fun wherever he went, and he always brought this feeling of no worries. Blake was going to be a father of a little boy, but the sea took away that chance.

Blake was closest to his mother, sister, brother, stepfather, and girlfriend; they were the ones who were hit hardest by this tragic accident. Even with their loss, the family was able to create light from the darkness of this tragedy. After mourning for some time, the close family founded the Blake Terry Memorial Foundation. This foundation shows how something as bad as losing a loved one can be turned into something good. The organization was founded by Blake's mother, stepfather, sister, and brother with donations from several businesses and families. The organization holds fishing rodeos and raises funds through donations to rescue and recover divers lost at sea. This organization is an important part of the system used to saving someone who is lost at sea; this foundation maybe the difference between life and death.

Try to picture being lost in the middle of nowhere with no food or water; you have nothing but your gear, if you're lucky. You are no longer near the safety of land; you have to swim to keep yourself alive. This isn't like swimming in your pool; picture waves that are five feet tall crashing into you while you're trying to keep yourself afloat. Picture being sucked under these waves and being tossed around like a child's rag doll; then the sea might spit you up or it might not. The ocean is a dangerous place that will take everything away from you if you make a mistake. When you're lost in the ocean, you have no sense of where you are, and the only thing that you have is the hope that someone is looking for you. Hope can push you on even when your body has given up on you. Hope can be the difference between an icy grave and a warm bed. If you don't believe that help will come, then you will give up and the sea will win its fight over you. This organization is that hope, and they will search for people until they have run out of options.

Blake Terry's family will always fight to keep this from happening to another family. The Blake Terry Memorial Foundation will always be waiting for the call to help someone who is lost at sea. The loss of Blake Terry will never be forgotten, but I think this accident will turn the world into a safer place. Some light can always come from darkness, and this is shown by the creation of the Blake Terry Memorial Foundation. Blake may be gone, but now he has become a guardian.

Guardian of the Gulf

Chapter 55

Even Pirates Go to Heaven

By Cindie Roussel

When Blake died on August 13, 2011, nothing and I mean nothing ever prepared me for the next year that I would go through. So many refer you to counseling not that I am against it, but you don't want to hear any suggestions, you just want that person back in your life. You want answers on when the hole in your heart will start healing. You want to know what the end to the story will be as what is happening to you seems to be so unreal. You want answers that no one can give you. I started to read books looking for answers. One book opened my eyes to what I hoped Blake felt passing from earth to heaven. The book gave an experience of someone dying and coming back to earth. What a great inspiration to read as I did not want to read about grief and understand it. I hated the word "grief." I hated this club that I was forced to join of people who had lost a child. I was now in their club. I hated it. I wanted to know what Blake was experiencing, not me! Then I read another book about losing a spouse while being pregnant. I wanted to try to understand what Rachel was going through being pregnant and losing the man she loved while carrying his child. I thought that I had to rescue her and keep her going as she was so fragile with his child, his precious child. This woman tells her story of everything she went through in her own unique way. I loved it as I thought a lot like her. I wanted to tell people that you have no idea how painful losing Blake was to us all. We are a great family and this kind of crap does not happen to a great family like us. We love each other, we believe in God, we all work hard and we do for others. We do the right things and this just does not happen to good people.

Then reality sets in. Blake is gone. The days go by and I burst into tears at any time or moment. I was standing in a local store having photos printed when I start to go through them, one of Blake is in the stack. I burst into tears right there. How do you explain this to the poor lady behind the counter? You can't. You just grab your stuff and run as quickly as you can.

I think for the first year, I ran. I hated parties and gatherings because I knew that everyone looked at me different. I would get a wave of depression from missing Blake and I had to just stay in bed. But then something strange started to happen. Everyone was having these dreams that seemed to be our connection to Blake. He continued to come to so many that I could not keep up with the stories so I started writing them down. Then he started coming to me in dreams. Each dream was special and so real. Words that Blake said were only those that only he would have said. You could hear him as though he was right there.

One day, I was heading to counseling and out of the blue, I heard "Cook Chicken-n-dumplings." Now I am already a basket case, heading for counseling and I am hearing voices? "Okay, Cindie...you are headed for the nut house," I thought! Only one person in my life would ask me to cook Chicken-n-dumplings and that would be Blake. Chicken-n-dumplings was Blake's favorite. He loved them and something about eating them always made you feel good inside. When I got to the counselor's office, I told her I could not stay long, I got to get home and cook. I called Whitney, Dustin, Rachel, Nobile, Jr., Nick, Joose and Boudreaux that I had a pot of Chicken-n- dumplings cooking. Blake wanted me to cook this for you. I think they all thought I had really lost it, but instead of making excuses to not show up, they all came over. Nobile had never had them and I can remember him telling me that they were awesome. They made him feel good inside. Hummmm...

Blake came to Jr. in many dreams but the last one, Jr. finally got to ask him something that had been bothering him. First he asked if he ever thought about one of them dying in the "Band of Brothers." Blake told him, "of course I did. I thought about it all the time." The second question he asked him was if he was happy. Blake told him, "What do you think? I get to see the big man every day!"

I think the most important dream that anyone has had is from a co-workers wife, Dawn Richard. We were at a Christmas party, December 11, 2012, almost 16 months since Blake's death. On the way to the party, I prayed to Blake that I wish I could hear from him. I prayed that he would give me a sign to let me know how he is doing. I just wanted to know that he was doing okay. At the party, Dawn and a good friend, Pam was sitting together at a table talking when I decided to join them. Pam asked me how I was doing and I told her that we are all doing really well. I truly meant that as I think as any family can survive such a loss and still be able to laugh and dance again, we cannot be doing too badly. I started to tell them how I stayed connected to Blake through dreams from others when Dawn's face turned white. She then said that she needed to tell me something. She told me of a dream she had recently, but just did not know how to approach me of this dream. She did not know Blake personally and she had never really met him. Only through pictures and family events that she remembered Blake. She said her dream was so real and that she first thought it was Whitney, my daughter in her dream but then she realized that it was Blake. She said that she first saw only the corner of his face. She said he then turned to her and just smiled. He said nothing to her. She said that he had this peaceful look on his face and he gave her this beautiful smile. She said the one thing that took her breath away was his wings. They were these beautiful large wings that she had never ever had such a vision before. He just looked deep into her eyes with this warm beautiful smile and then she suddenly woke up. She did not understand her dream and she wondered why he came to her in a dream. She did not know how to tell me. I just smiled as I tried to hold back the tears. Of all the dreams that everyone had shared with me, this was the first dream that anyone had told me that Blake had wings. "He made it!" I told her, with relief in my heart! "He made it to God's Kingdom! He is now an angel of God! He made it!!!" I kept telling her with tears in my eyes! How I am at peace that he is with God. This is the perfect ending to our story. God has a plan. He does not punish or take away, but is a forgiving God who loves us all. I had to learn to trust him with my child. I had to give everything I had over to him to trust that Blake would be okay. I am at peace with God now and I know Blake is okay. No, he is better than okay, he is now serving God and he had to share this with me.

On New Year's Eve 2012, I got a call from Korte Cheramie. He was crying so hard as he had dreamed of Blake that morning. Blake had come to him and told him that he loved him. He told him to please tell my Mom that I am okay. He told him over and over that Korte wanted to call me that morning, but waited. Finally after speaking to his Mom, Jill, he called me.

I am so grateful as Blake wanted me to know that he had earned his wings. He is now where he is supposed to be, with our Father. He is at peace as he needed to make sure we were all okay and he wanted me to know this.

Blake, I know you are safe and you are happy. I know that you are where you need to be. I love you, Mom!

"Jesus said to her, "Your brother will rise again." Martha said to him, "I know that he will rise again in the resurrection on the last day." Jesus said to her, "I am the resurrection and the life. Whoever believes in me, though he die, yet shall he live, and everyone who lives and believes in me shall never die. Do you believe this?" John 11:23-26

Chapter 56

Pecan Pie

By Cindie Roussel

"Who ate the pecans off the pecan pie?" was always heard at family gatherings. Then altogether everyone would shout at once, "BLAKE!" Blake was always doing something that stirred everyone up during the holidays. Whether he was eating all the pecans off the top of the pecan pies or passing out in his dinner plate because he went hunting that morning and drank too much whiskey to keep warm. You just never knew what to expect. So of course, I have another great story to share:

After Hurricane Katrina hit in August of 2005, I decided to invite my entire family from the Gulf Coast of Mississippi to spend the Thanksgiving Holidays with us. I knew that they were all trying to put their lives back together and trying to get into the spirit of the holidays were difficult to say the least. I spent my week preparing the list of food we would eat and all the trimmings. I rented tables and chairs as our house on Romy was not big enough for everyone so I decorated outside on our porch. Scott had built a porch across the front of our house and it was a perfect setting under our huge oak tree in the front yard. I had made table clothes and cushion covers to make the setting so elegant that I hoped that everyone would be comfortable.

That morning I was up at 5:00 to put the turkey in the oven and start preparing the meal. The house carried the aroma of turkey and dressing baking in the oven. I made the sweet potato casserole and started the peas. Our family gatherings were not complete without pecan pie. I had everything. I set the tables with my Christmas China and wine bottles and I had even decorated my Christmas tree as I wanted to really make the house festive. Earlier that morning, Blake had took- off to go hunting, something that he loved to do on Thanksgiving morning. I was not happy about him hunting as I wanted this to be a very special holiday with so many coming from the Gulf Coast, but he promised he would not be long so I let him go.

Deke, Jared, Blake and Nobile

As everyone arrived the house soon filled with laughter and music. My parents loved to sing so they sat outside on the porch playing old songs while everyone enjoyed their wine before dinner. As dinner time got closer, there was no sign of Blake. I began to get upset but I knew I should not have let him go and I could not let dinner get cold. I called everyone into eat. After everyone had a belly full, back out on the porch we went to listen to some more music when Blake finally arrived. He is two sheets to the wind as he had too much whiskey that morning hunting with his buddies, Deke, Nobile and Jared. I thought, GREAT, here we had everyone at the house, and he walks in from drinking all morning. Frustrated, I told him to go eat some dinner to sober up. He hugged me and told me he loved me then he swayed into the kitchen. Not long after Blake sat down to eat his plate piled with all the fixin's Dustin walked in to only find Blake's face planted into his plate passed-out. Dustin said, "Dude, wake up. You better get up before Mom sees you." Blake lifted his head with sweet potato all over his face and stumbled to his bed room. Fortunately, I never saw this or did any of my family. But the one thing we all remember that year was when it came time to eat the pecan pie, there were no pecans on the pie.

After that Christmas holiday, I started a tradition of buying pecan pies at the Cajun Pecan House in Cutoff for my family and friends. It was something that we all come to laugh about with Blake eating the pecans off the pie that year. Then it changed to where Blake started delivering the pies for me. As the week of Christmas would approach, he would say, "Mah, you ordered my pies yet?" Funny, I bought the pies and yet he delivered them as a gift from him. Hummm..He was pretty slick but he loved giving them. Each would laugh as they knew the story behind the pecan pie but loved getting them as there were no other pies like the Cajun Pecan House Pies.

The Christmas following Blake's death, I had forgotten about ordering his pies and Christmas was approaching when I heard a voice in my head, "Mah, you ordered my pies yet?" I froze as it had completely slipped my mind. I stopped what I was doing and called right away to order his pies. That year, Terry, my sister and I drove to each house, delivering Blake's Pecan Pies.

Family traditions and holidays are not easy to continue after losing that special someone in your life. Our holidays were filled with food, drinks and plenty of laughter. But all that seemed to change as it was so hard to celebrate the holidays without Blake. All I can tell is that time does heal and new traditions will come. This past Christmas, three years later, we had not planned a lot to do as I told my children to start building their own traditions and Scott and I will join them in whatever they would like to do.

Christmas Eve morning, Katy called me to see what I was doing. Scott left for work and I was drinking coffee still in my pajamas. She asked if they could come over for breakfast. Dustin wanted to cook pancakes. As it turned out, everyone came over that morning and we sat around in our pajamas drinking coffee and eating pancakes and bacon. After everyone went back to their homes to get dressed to head out for last minute shopping, I decided to bake cookies for all of Blake's friends as this was something I always did since they were kids. The house still smelled of bacon and syrup as I started drinking eggnog listening to Christmas music, I prayed to Blake at his shrine and I hoped he could hear me as I missed him so much. I told him how hard it still was as we were all doing our best to keep going. I prayed that he would help us build a new beginning of traditions. I told him that I loved him "This much" and I asked God to protect him. Then I sat there, crying as I missed him so much.

That evening, Daniel walked in with a huge iron pot and the rest of the crew followed. Whitney turned to me and said, "Mom, Daniel wants to start a new tradition! He wants to cook sauce picante for Christmas Eve." I froze and then I just smiled as I knew that this was a gift from Blake. He heard me crying and he knew he needed to help ease my pain. Later that evening I hugged Daniel as tight as I could. I told him that I thanked God every day for bringing him into our lives and that Blake must have sent him a message because he just answered my prayers.

"If there is a physical body, there is
also a spiritual body. Lo! I tell you
a mystery. We shall not all sleep,
but we shall all be changed, in a
moment, in the twinkling of an
eye, at the last trumpet."
1 Corinthians 15: 44, 51

Chapter 57

The Circle of Life

By Cindie Roussel

There is no hurt stronger than losing a child. So many people told me that they could not imagine losing a child. I would just tell them to not try to imagine such a loss. The pain is unbearable and why would you even try to put yourself in my shoes? The pain was so deep that I had these feelings in the lower part of my diaphragm as if I were having contractions. A feeling of aching as I did when I was pregnant with my children. It dawned on me that it was feelings like of carrying a child in my womb. The bible relates so much to a mother's womb. Then it dawned on me that a Mother is still connected to her child even in death because she holds the birthplace of that child. Our connection starts in our womb and when we lose a child, we can feel the loss of that connection through our womb. Do you know how many times the mother's womb is mentioned in the bible? Think about it...this is no coincidence that this connection is more than we realize. We also do not realize the bigger picture of life when going through such a loss. Scott and I began to realize how our lives needed to change. We needed to live more and stop planning for what may never happen. I don't mean not to plan for retirement or build up savings for a rainy day. I mean that we both may not be here tomorrow so we better make sure we are preparing just in case. Get your suits ready! We all believe that we will go on as if we plan to grow old together. Our children were looking forward to having children together. Sharing becoming parents and watching their children grow-up as they did. Then something like this happens and now they don't have Blake here to be the Paran of their children. They don't have Blake here to be the best-man or the brother to lean-on for advice. The "Team Terry Racing Team" is no longer a team. Losing Blake made us all realize that we need to live more in the moment then in the future. We don't know what the future brings so we better grab what we can now.

We are all closer now as a family since Blake has been gone. We spend nights and weekends cooking out and enjoying each other's company. Scott finally bought the boat he always dreamed of and I bought an in-ground swimming pool for my 50th birthday. We moved Whitney and Daniel into Blake's house and moved Dustin and Katy behind them. Everyone is together. Rachel and Hank visit just about every weekend. We have become so close that we make sure everyone is included in our plans. Last night, we celebrated the announcement of another child joining our family as Whitney is pregnant again. This time, I am not so out of it that I can enjoy the excitement.

As everyone was sitting in the sunroom, I took a moment to look around the room at the talking and noise of the grandchildren playing. Rachel and Hank are curled up on the big lounger. Katy and Dustin are on the sofa with Austin playing with his race track. Daniel is sitting at the table with Scott and Adrienne is coloring on the floor. Whitney is trying to talk with Rachel and Cameron was fussy as he was not ready for bed and he was not letting her talk. I reached for him and he wrapped his arms around me. We went into the living room where it was quiet and I rocked him gently as I sang, "You are my sunshine." I sang this song every night to Blake when he was a baby. Cameron looked up at me and he slowly closed his eyes. I looked over at Blake's candle as it glowed beneath his picture. I smiled at Blake and I thanked God for his beautiful blessings as well as helping me breathe again. I thanked him for giving me my family hope again by giving us all these beautiful children. I thanked him for giving me the time with Blake and that I hoped he will keep him close to us all. I thanked him for all those who have been there for us and most of all, for this baby I was holding in my arms. Life does go on and we need to embrace every moment. We need to trust in God's plan as he loves us. He understands our sacrifices as he is a merciful God. He gave us the ultimate sacrifice, his only son, Jesus. I had to do the same with Blake. I have a different relationship with God because of this. I finally had to learn to trust in God again. I can't give you the answers as to when the pain will subside when losing someone you love as I still break down at the drop of a hat. However, I can tell you that it does get better over time. Trust in God...trust in him and he will give you what you need to survive anything. The circle of life will continue and you must always embrace every moment as though it were your last!

EVEN PIRATES GO TO HEAVEN

(A Message from Blake in a Dream that came to me)

Little pig, little pig, let me in
Not by the hair of my chinny, chinny, chinny
Then I'll huff and I'll puff and I'll BLOOOWWW your house in
As he let out a roar and threw back his chin…

He bent down on one knee
…with his arms open wide
Give Captain BT a hug
So I climbed up on his side…

Let me tell you a story
I am not the wolf that I pretend to be
I am merely a Pirate
That was lost at sea…

His hair was golden
With sapphire blue eyes
His wings were so soft and big
That his arches seem to touch the sky…

I'm fighting the demons, he said…
At the first of morning light
I'm searching for treasures by day,
And dancing with the maidens under the moonlight…

He let out a laugh…
That almost knocked me off his knee
Then he pulled me close
And whispered, listen…listen to me…

Life is like the water
It can change as fast as the wind
When you feel like your sinking
Just reach out and I will give you my hand…

Being good is not easy
So please promise me that you will try to be
For even Pirates go to Heaven
That is my promise to you from me…

*"Let not your hearts be troubled. Believe in God;
believe also in me. In my Father's house are
many rooms. If it were not so, would I have told
you that I go to prepare a place for you? And if I
go and prepare a place for you, I will come again
and will take you to myself, that where I am you
may be also." John 14:1-4*

Chapter 58

You Are My Sunshine

By Cindie Roussel

The following pages are from my daily journal during the hardest days of my life. Each day I prayed and I spoke to Blake to help me breathe again. I wrote these pages and sometimes letters to Blake as I missed him so much. Through Blake and God's love, I am healing. I could not have made it through all of this without Blake's "Band of Brothers." I love them so much and I am grateful that I had 27 beautiful years with Blake. I hope through my journey and others, you find that heaven and earth are not so far apart. I hope that through Blake's connection with me, we are able to restore your faith and bring you hope. Believe in God's promise!

Boudreaux, Joose, Cindie, Hank, Ponce, Dustin, Jr. and T.C.

Even Pirates Go to Heaven

A Mother's Memoirs

September 2011
(The First Month)

September 6ᵗʰ, 2011 - Life is standing still with the death of Blake. My heart is so heavy and I keep asking why? Why Blake? What did I do to cause this pain? Is my faith not strong enough Lord? I don't know what to pray anymore. I was so blessed just a few days ago and now it seems all is gone. How I look at each day differently. What am I supposed to do? Work and normal routines are just not possible. I look at pictures and try to find peace but my heart is heavy as I know he is not coming back. How empty I feel.

September 7ᵗʰ, 2011 - Today is a crisp cool morning and I prayed all the way to work. I prayed for Blake's soul to be released. I prayed that he is already sitting on the right of our God and he has been purified in the blood of the lamb. I also believe that I need to work harder with myself in preparing my path. I am not sure if there is such a thing as purgatory, but I do believe there is some process of purification before facing God. I pray God is protecting Blake and keeping him safe.

September 8th, 2011 - Today is another cool fall morning, weather was 59º. We had Nobile, Deek, Hunter, Dustin & kids, Whit & Daniel over last night. Whit told everyone she is pregnant. It is exciting, but my heart is so empty that it will take time to feel happy again. Not the reaction I know Whit expected. Blake has to be in Heaven as the devil is making me question and test my faith. He is with Jesus and I know it. I have to believe this. Timmy lost his sister this week and I know Blake is with her now. Blake is making our path as he did for us to go to Grand Isle. He recognized beauty and God's works. I will try to follow his path, no more "Martha, Martha!" I will love and try to enjoy life more.

September 14th, 2011 - I did not write anything yesterday as it was 1 month since Blake's accident. I had an okay day, but felt bad late last night. I dreamed a lot about Blake. Working on Foundation things and trying to stay busy. I just wish I could get back to some kind of normalcy but just don't know how. I miss him terribly and I don't know what more to do. There is nothing...absolutely nothing to take this pain away!

September 15, 2011 - Today I am in physical pain as I got my tattoo yesterday. Yes, I can't believe I got a tattoo. I miss my Blake so much. I just feel lost and hoping he will call me on the phone. Lord I pray you have him next to you giving him strength and courage to go on without us as we need the strength and courage without him. I know I have to trust in you to protect him. I am not sure how we will go on without him. Please forgive me for doubting you and release me from the devil.

September 19th, 2011 - Everything takes such an EFFORT!!! NOTHING MORE TO SAY TODAY!!!

September 20th, 2011 - I find rest in God, only he can give me hope. Psalms 62
I can't let the devil continue to bring me to the dark side of Blake's death. I think of him and how lost I am without him.

I cannot help Rachel, Nobile, Whit and Dustin without God's Grace. Blake, please stay close to me and give me guidance. I am so lost.
I love you, son! Mom

September 22nd, 2011 - Yesterday I could not get out of bed. I need change as my life feels so empty. Blake is speaking to my heart telling me o take care of everyone. We need to pull together to find ourselves again. Blake took care of all of us and he wants me to do this for him. I know he is trying so hard to comfort us all. God PLEASE grant me the strength and courage.

September 26th, 2011 - Today I am too sick to get out of bed. I don't want to be here. Work is so hard. It takes so much effort. I pray that I can get up one morning and be excited about life. I am going to join a couple of chat sites to help with grieving. I am not real excited about counseling as it does not seem to help.

September 27th, 2011 - Blake, I felt your presence this morning and I heard you. You told me that heaven is like you told us when we were little. It is like climbing in a bed of fresh sheets. I love you and miss you, Blake! Please keep close to me and help me to be able to help others. Show me the path. Give me signs for me to continue my strength and warm my heart. Don't leave me!!! I know God has work for you but PLEASE stay close.

I love you, Mom.

(The Following Months)

October 13ᵗʰ, 2011

Today marks the second month of Blake's death. I can't seem to keep focused as my heartaches so much. Blake's friends are really wonderful and they are trying to do so much. He was truly blessed and so are we. I continue to ask God to keep Jesus in my heart and keep my thoughts clear so that I can join my baby in Heaven. I miss you, kiddo! Love Mom

November 13ᵗʰ, 2011

It is hard to believe that yesterday marked three months. I miss Blake so much these days. I hope I can look back at the great memories of him without feeling so empty. I hope Blake will stay close to me. I hope that God will protect him from being lost. I hope...I hope...I hope!

December 13ᵗʰ, 2011

Today makes four months that our lives changed forever. Tears continue to fall and the emptiness is so deep. I miss you so much. We are all trying so hard to keep going. I continue to ask you for signs to let me know you are there. I know God will keep us together somehow. I have to keep the faith. I hope you are at peace and I hope you don't hurt like we do.
I love you baby! Mom
P.S. We find out today if Whitney is having a boy or girl!

January 13th, 2012

Dear Blake I am listening to "How Great Thou Art." I know God is protecting you and he is building your work as there is nothing you cannot do without him. I hope you are happy and smiling as today marks five months you left us all. We miss you so much. I promise to do what I can to keep your spirit alive and do God's will so that we will be together again. I love you so much. Today is another special day as it is Rachel's birthday. The Lord is our rock and salvation, it is well my soul! I love you, Mom.

February 13th, 2012

Today marks six months since Blake's death. Our world is different without him here. I tell myself to keep moving just keep moving. The tears will never stop and the memories will never go away. I know we all have a purpose. Dipping deep in our souls looking for that answer is just not that easy. When your soul search, the pain hits you that he is gone. Never to be the same. Never to have those moments again. All we have is our memories.

We have to have faith that the moments will come again. God's promise to us.

March 21ˢᵗ, 2012

Good Morning, Sweetie! Happy Birthday! I miss you so much! I have to be strong for the rest of the crew as I know you are counting on me. I broke down when it hit me that you would be 28 years old today. The words "would be" hit hard...I know you are very much alive in our hearts and in the spiritual world. God has you in heaven taking care of those who need help. Today we will celebrate your new life in Christ! I love you, Mom

Blake's 27th Birthday
(His last birthday we celebrated together)

April 13ᵗʰ, 2012

Dear Blake, How I miss you so much. I don't sleep and I drink too much wine in the evenings. Constant voices in my head with me dreaming all night. I feel so lost. I know you are safe with God but I can't help but miss you. Time keeps rolling almost too fast that I feel I am having to hang on. I pray every day for you to have your wings and you are helping others as I know that is what you love. I know you will do well in heaven. God will protect you. I need strength to keep going. I love you, Mom!

May 15ᵗʰ, 2012

Dear Son, Yesterday made nine months you left us. Dustin and I shared what your last words with each of us. It seemed unreal as we still see you in dreams and we talk but your last words to me were the Thursday when you left out. You said, "I love you, Mom." Nobile told me that if you both aren't back by Sunday to call the Coast Guard.

Dustin said that the last time he talked to you was a phone call you made to him while he was at work. You called him and started singing a song to him. He told you that he could not talk and you both laughed, and hung up.

Whitney struggled to remember her last conversation with you but then she remembered a text message. She wanted to know if you wanted her Saints tickets. You said, No- that you were going fishing.

We lost you that Saturday. How I wish you would have stayed back. I know your love was the water and the excitement of catching that big grouper. We miss you so much.

Yesterday was another sad day as Aaron Autin lost his mother. Please watch for her, Blake. Give Aaron comfort if you can. We Love you, Mom!

June 13ᵗʰ, 2012

Blake, today is so crazy. Dustin and I are trying to get things moving for the Foundation. You must be proud of everyone. I miss you so much. You seem so far away now. I try to block the empty and just keep moving forward. Nothing can fill that hole. I keep believing that we will be together again and you are preparing my path for me. I hope you are not lonely or feel any sorrow. I hope you are happy and you can continue to provide hope to all of us here! We struggle daily at our missing you. We miss you so much! I love you, Mom!

July 13ᵗʰ, 2012

Blake, today marks eleven months that you have been gone. I miss you terribly. We cope in our own ways but we grieve together. I hate the word - grieve!
Dustin, Whitney, Scott and I seem to be doing okay. It is hard some days and other days we get by. Today the Sea-Quest is offshore with some of the same crew fishing in the Oilman's Rodeo. It is rainy and seems to me not enough rain could measure the tears I have cried this year. I

promise to you to keep smiling and pull myself out of this despair, but I need your help! I love you, Mom!

August 13th, 2012

I miss you, kiddo! We are at one year and the pain is still so strong. I have lost my eyelashes and I look like hell! I get up, go to work and try to get through each day knowing that you aren't here. I think of you constantly. I pray you are in Paradise and you feel only happiness. I hope you are with us at all our happy moments. I love you, Mom!

September 13th, 2012

Thinking of you so much! I cried all day yesterday as my heart ached so much. After a year, the tears don't stop. I pray you can look on us and give us guidance. I know Rachel struggles too.

I am so grateful I have Scott. Never did we think we would go through this as a family. I hope you are okay. I love you, Mom!

October 13th, 2012

Dear Blake, I don't cry as much. I don't write to you as much, either. Life seems to move at a pace so fast and busy that it seems to have gotten away from me. Hank is getting so big and so is Cameron. I hope you can see Wildman (Austin). He is going to give both Hank and Cameron trouble. Ms. Adrienne misses you and we talk about you all the time. I know you can see them and talk to them. God has the secret of how babies can communicate with the angels. I think about you every second of the day and I wonder how you are doing. Please let me know through our way of communicating. I miss you! Here I go...crying again! I love you, Mom!

November 13th, 2012

Dear Son, every day you are on my mind. I wake up thinking about you and I go to sleep hoping to see you in my dreams. I thought this morning how life really does go on. How each of your friends are now finding their paths. How proud I am of Dustin and Whitney. How blessed to have a wonderful husband and a house full of grandchildren. How blessed that Katy, Daniel and Rachel have joined our family. Thank God for giving us YOU to be a part of our lives. I know you are with me! I love you and I miss you so much, Mom!

December 13th, 2012

Blake, it has been several months since I wrote in my journal. Holidays are so tough, I am trying to get into the spirit. Sometimes I just get overwhelmed feeling so lost without you that I fall apart. Then, I feel your presence. I know you are with me and that comforts me. I just wish I could see you walk in that door and tell me, "Hey, Mah!" I miss you so much!

We are all doing good, which only confirms to me that you are watching out for all of us. I pray for you daily and I need your big arms around me. I love you, Mom!

January 13ᵗʰ, 2013

Dear Blake, I miss you so much. Every day I pray you are doing okay and happy. I miss hearing your voice and laughter. You can't even imagine I am sure. I had Blake, Jr. this weekend and little things he would do reminded me of you. I know he knows you as he looks at me as though he is telling me through his eyes. He has the prettiest eyes. They are the color of Grandpa Chester eyes. The color of the ocean. He has that beautiful blonde top just like yours. I could just imagine you walking around with him in your arms. I know God has a plan and every day I am seeing more and more of new things that he is wanting me to see and do. I Love you and MISS you so Much, Mom!

February 13ᵗʰ, 2013

Dear Blake, yesterday was a rough day for me as all I thought about was valentines when I would buy your heart candy and you would re-give to whom-ever you decided at the time. You sure loved giving! Ha! I miss you every day and Blake Jr. is growing so fast. He turns those eyes at me and I can see your spirit in him. Rachel is having a tough time, but I know you are watching over her. I love you, Mom!

March 13ᵗʰ, 2013

Dear Blake, I think we are doing better. WE are stronger and closer and ready to do more. We lean on each other more than before. I am so grateful God has allowed us to stay close to you. I know none of us could have survived if we would not had the chance to dream of you. You gave so much to each of us that you must know it was the only way for us to have peace. I love you and I miss you so much. I am comforted to know you are with me always! I love you, Mom!

April 13th, 2013

Hey kiddo, I miss you so much that I think I cried all day yesterday. I really miss you to talk with. I miss you and Nobile hanging out in the barn. I miss you coming through the back door, shouting, "Hey Mah, what's for supper?" I put a pool across the yard where you walked. I hoped it would make me feel better, but it doesn't. I miss you so much. I pray you are doing well. I pray you are happy. I hope to see more of you soon. I just want to hug you! I just can't fight the emptiness. I hope you can see all the kids and enjoy your son, Blake Jr. I love you, Mom!

May 2nd, 2013

Dear Kiddo, Time is moving at a fast pace as always. I have barely anytime to stop and reflect on where I am in life. I stare at your picture and I still cannot believe you are gone from us. I turn 50 next week and I know you would be giving me so much grief. The kids gave me a wonderful party and we danced like there was not tomorrow. I know you are dancing with Rose and Celeste. I know you and Grandpa Chester are analyzing what work you and him need to be doing next. I love you, Mom

June 6ʰ, 2013
(Last Journal Entry)

Hey Sweetie! Well, Sissy (Whitney) is pregnant again. The Circle of Life continues. I hope you are happy! I hope you are enjoying your new journey with God. I miss you! I love you, Mom!

"You are my sunshine
My only sunshine
You make me happy
When skies are grey
You'll never know dear
How much I love you
So don't take my sunshine away."

Even Pirates Go to Heaven

Meet the Author

Cindie Roussel

The Mother of pirate, Captain BT, tells her story of raising him, teaching him and most of all LOVING him!

Cindie and her husband, Scott live in Thibodaux, Louisiana. She is the mother of three and grandmother of five now. While she was writing this book, her fifth grandchild was born, Lily Marie.

REFERENCES

Buffet, Jimmy. "A Pirate Looks at Forty"; "Why don't we get drunk and screw"; "Pencil Thin Mustache". Songs You Know by Heart. January 1985 as MCA 5633.

Chesney, Kenny. "Out Last Night". The Greatest Hits II. April 6, 2009.

"Leave It To Beaver". The show was created by writers Joe Connelly and Bob Mosher. CBS on October 4, 1957.

MercyMe. "I Can Only Imagine". Mercy Me is a contemporary Christian group. Written by Bart Millard. 2001

Strait, George. "Here for a Good Time". Here for a Good Time. Co-written with son Bubba and songwriter Dean Dillon, was released in June 2011.

"The Ladies Man". Written by Tim Meadows, Dennis McNicholas, Andrew Steele. Released June 28th, 1961.

Young, Chris. "Gettin' You Home". The Man I Want to Be. February 2009.

"You Are My Sunshine" first recorded in 1939. It has been declared one of the state songs of Louisiana as a result of its association with former state governor and country music singer Jimmie Davis. The song is copyright 1940 Peer International Corporation, words and music by Jimmie Davis and Charles Mitchell.

Please visit our website
www.piratesgotoheaven.com